Heal Your Birth Story
...releasing the unexpected

Maureen Campion

DEDICATION

First I thought there was only my story. Sharing my story allowed me to hear other stories, and through their stories came my growth and healing.

CONTENTS

PREFACE

The Journey to Resolving Your Birth Story

This book is part of my personal healing birth story. I wrote this book for the women who courageously, generously, passionately shared their unspeakable stories with me. I wrote this book for the women holding unspeakable stories yet to be told.

As women and as mothers, we have a complicated relationship with birth. Creating life with one's own body is transformational. Cells, then blob, then something fish like, then the baby that looks like a chicken. The chicken grows hair and fingernails and you get that it is part you and part not you, but the baby can only grow inside of one person—the person who someday must birth this new life. There is the ever-present thought that this foreign creature that you have allowed to inhabit your body for nine months must come out. There is no denying it. The baby has to come out. Before names and onesies, there will be a birth.

Women prepare for birth. Some spend hours on the Internet. Some take classes and monitor their diet and do yoga and meditate. Some place themselves in the hands of experts and look for others to decide. Some deny and ignore and bury their head in the sand...but they too are preparing. We want our births to be safe. We want our babies to be healthy. We want our experience to be uncomplicated and predictable. We don't really expect it to be painless but we want to be brave and dignified as we face the pain. For most women, if we could, we would have it be beautiful. Soft and serene and peaceful and loving and magical.

That is how we picture birth. That is how they sell it. Prepare, get ready, be brave, and you get to have a beautiful, safe, manageable birth. For the vast majority of modern social media mommas, within days or weeks of giving birth, you post your birth story. A birth story has become part of the ritual. Your friends expect to hear the story. We measure by hours, sometimes by days. We count stitches and list interventions. We share Apgar scores, birth weights, and breast feeding struggles.

There is a dark side to birth. There are stories that are painful, if not impossible to tell. Each year nearly 15% of U.S. women, at least 200,000 women, report feeling traumatized by their birth. Between 2-6% of U.S. women are so troubled after their births that they meet the criteria for full-blown Post Traumatic Stress Disorder, a mental health disorder shared with combat soldiers and rape victims. Over 200,000 women a year have a birth story that isn't easy to talk about. Their story seems wrong. It feels shameful or raw or a mistake. It is not the story they expected.

In 2001, when I was pregnant with my second child, I had to face my own birth trauma. Once I opened the dark closet of my own story, it got easier to talk to other mommas. As a psychologist and specialist in postpartum mood issues, women started sharing their birth stories with me. As a friend, I started asking, "So how was it?" and really listening. In 2007 my colleague and fellow survivor, Sarina LaMarch and I created our "Healing Birth Stories" workshop. The book, *Healing Your Birth Story* follows from that work, and I believe it provides valuable tools to move past emotional distress to an empowered relationship with your birth story and your body.

How I got here.

I have a bachelor's degree in Psychology and a master's degree in Marriage and Family Therapy. I didn't learn about birth trauma in school. I had never read a book about it. I actually had never heard the term before I was pregnant for the third time. Ten years ago I asked my friend Susan Lane for her help in finding a birth provider who could help me to have a VBAC (vaginal birth after cesarean) at my AMA (Advanced Maternal Age of 38). Susan was a friend and an experienced doula. I told her I wanted a vaginal birth and needed her help. Her first question was, "Have you done any work to deal with your birth trauma?"

I remember that I rolled the term "birth trauma" around in my head for a moment or two. I hadn't talked much about my first birth but I must have told her something. Birth trauma? Out of nowhere I burst into sobs. A wound burst open. Oh, I had birth trauma.

So the journey began.

I will share all of my birth stories with you, but hang in there...not just yet.

Here I was, a licensed psychologist running a treatment program for the naughtiest of teenage boys in the Twin Cities. I had read tons of books about birth and tons of books about trauma, but not once had those two words ever occurred in the same sentence. They had certainly never been used about my surgical birth. I don't like the term cesarean section or c-sect. Doctors use the term section to describe what is done to a woman. "She was sectioned." Hate that word. I prefer surgical birth and vaginal birth. In 16 years I had never spoken in depth of my birth experience. I had not even discussed it with my mother who had been there with me as my birth support person. I had never even returned to the doctor for my six-week postpartum visit. I had closed the book on that experience. I had a healthy baby. I *got over it*. I thought.

Preparing for my second birth (there is another story—a first trimester miscarriage, too), I dove head first into birth trauma work only because I thought it gave me a shot at a better outcome for my pregnancy. If I was going to avoid another traumatic birth, I knew things had to be examined. I wouldn't have dug around in there, opened this can of worms for any other reason. I would never have unlocked that pain. I wasn't even aware it existed. I simply cut myself off from birth and my feelings and my experience and figured it was over and done with. Time hadn't healed anything or I wouldn't have felt so raw. This didn't feel like visiting hurt from my past, it felt like ripping the scab off and having it all festering right there. I have no idea what covering my pain was costing me. I don't remember exactly, but I know that I was impatient with other women's birth stories. I trivialized surgical birth. I trivialized the great stories too. I didn't want to talk about anyone's birth. Because I never asked, I never heard about anyone's birth trauma. Unresolved trauma left me less present to emotional pain and limited my access to healing. The work of resolving my personal trauma has made a world of difference to the work I do with others.

Since first being introduced to the world of birth trauma, I have started my own psychology and marriage counseling practice focused on the years of transition, of becoming parents. I have worked a great deal with women who struggle with postpartum mood disorders-postpartum anxiety and depression. During this time, I have also given birth to my two youngest sons, become actively engaged with the amazing world of natural birth, and the attachment parenting community. And each step of the way I have allowed the women in my life to teach me about birth by asking them to share their stories with me. I can hear the amazing, thrilling, happy stories and I can hear the ones that start with, "I'm fine," then dissolve into tears and tough truths. There are many stories that require an especially receptive audience, that take time and compassion to share.

I will share my own personal birth story. I will share my first birth in 1984, Nate's "emergency" surgical birth under general anesthesia. I will share the short, sad story of a 10-week pregnancy that I lost. I will share my second birth in 2002, Joey's "failed VBAC attempt" and lovely surgical birth; and I will share my third and final birth in 2004, Zach's "VBA2C," vaginal birth after two cesareans.

For some women, knowing my story will help you to trust that I know what you've been dealing with, but for others it is hard not to compare and contrast your story with mine or anyone else's. I know that not all women get the chance to resolve their trauma by having another baby. I don't want to hold my journey up as the best or only way to resolve trauma. It's up to you to decide if you read it first or last or never. The short version, just the facts, are that when Nate was born I felt horrible about his birth. I ignored it and I thought that it didn't matter. I didn't know that my struggles with breast feeding were associated with my trauma. I didn't know that Nate was impacted by this birth. I didn't know that it would impact every other birth decision I would ever make. I also ignored that by locking myself away from my own birth story, I was unable to hear and honor all women's stories. If mine was "fine," then all stories were equal. "Fine" doesn't allow for trauma but it also doesn't allow for triumph or ecstasy or empowerment or beauty. In my mind, birth only equaled outcome and the only measure was the baby, not the mother, not the relationship.

When my doula named my pain, she offered me access to healing. As a psychologist I had a great deal of experience in how to heal trauma. I had worked with

11

people who had been abused or raped or betrayed in some way. I went in search of the support I assumed would be out there. I looked for books or groups or even articles. I found there was nothing. In fact, I now know that the term *birth trauma* was first used by Kathleen Kendall-Tackett in 1992 in a professional article, "Postpartum Depression: A Comprehensive Approach for Nurses." The study of birth trauma was, and in many ways still is, in its infancy.

I found other women who felt traumatized by birth, but no ideas on how to help them. I grew increasingly frustrated with the lack of resources. I wanted to talk about my journey. I wanted to hear other women's stories. I wanted to know what was normal, what healing should look like, and that I was not alone.

"Someone should do a workshop." I approached doulas and childbirth educators and midwives and other therapists. I knew at least five different childbirth education programs here in the Twin Cities, but no one wanted to touch birth trauma. "Someone should do a workshop." I wanted the birth professionals to take this on. I wanted someone who believed in the power and significance of natural birth to take this on. And though everyone agreed there was a need, and people gave a lot of lip service to understanding the need, no one knew where to start. It became clear that if a birth trauma workshop was going to happen, I would need to invent it first. With my friend and colleague Sarina LaMarche (www.mybalancedlife.com), who was working through her own birth loss and trauma story, we began to offer

12

"Healing Birth Stories" workshops in the Twin Cities starting in 2006.

Honestly I remember asking Sarina to help me because I was terrified of what would happen if we got a room of women to talk about what they had all been afraid to talk about. I thought we might have women fall apart. I thought they might not be able to compassionately hear each others' stories. But somehow we knew. We knew or we never would have started. We knew that the only way to learn how to help women heal trauma was from the women themselves. We knew that the best thing for women to do was to share their birth stories. It was what set us apart. We were those women who didn't talk about our births. And never once has a woman fallen apart or been harshly judged. We use a lot of Kleenex, but each woman finds something powerful in her sharing.

The workshops gave me back my love and my passion for natural birth. The workshops taught me how to heal and forgive and learn from the things that happen to us when things are beyond our control. This book comes from our work together and from the courageous women who felt compelled to share their stories and their healing. I have asked them to allow me to honor the work that they have done by integrating their stories into my book. I will offer their stories in their own words with their permission, changing names and details to protect their privacy. It is my wish that this book offer support and guidance to all women who feel unresolved, disappointed, or wounded by their births. As we heal our stories, we make ourselves available to the world of empowered birth.

Chapter 1
Is This Book for Me?

If we are to heal the planet, we must begin by healing birthing.

-Agnes Sallet Von Tannenberg

You know your birth story is unresolved if you:
* become emotionally overwhelmed talking about your birth
* avoid hearing other women's birth stories
* dismiss your own feelings about your birth and have to keep telling yourself that you're "fine"
* shut down when the topic of birth comes up
* obsess about the details of your birth and find it intruding on your thoughts

Many women struggle to express how they feel about their birth. For me, the term birth trauma has been a powerful piece of my healing. It isn't necessary for you to feel connected to that term in order to use this book to work through your own birth story. If you feel angry, frustrated, resentful, disappointed, violated, or wounded by your birth or your pregnancy loss, *Healing Your Birth Story* will help you understand those feelings and move forward in your recovery. That's it. It doesn't have to be bad enough, or a certain kind of horror, or have a specific outcome. *Healing Your Birth Story* is for you if you want to work through some of the complicated feelings you have about your birth story.

The participants in our workshop walk through the door worried that their experience isn't the "right" kind of story. If they had a cesarean, they were told it was to save their life or the lives of their babies. If they had a natural birth, they feel guilty complaining because they are thrilled that they didn't have a cesarean. If they birthed at home beautifully and ended up transferred to the hospital for complications it is hard to reconcile the beautiful moments from the scariest ones. I have never heard a "good" birth story that didn't have a few crazy, scary, intense moments. I have never heard a birth trauma story that didn't have a few wonderful, miraculous moments. Birth is complicated.

In the legal world, birth trauma means something physically damaging happened, usually to the baby. And if something bad happened, someone is responsible. Someone messed up. Birth trauma = lawsuits. Most of us have more experience thinking of trauma as physical harm. We think about ERs and war zones. We think of trauma as something that leaves visible scars.

Psychological trauma is damage to the psyche that occurs as a result of a severely distressing event. Trauma is a wound to your spirit, to your emotions, to your sense of yourself. You can tell it is trauma when, over time, the story continues to feel unfinished. A traumatic memory feels alive, raw, or stuck. When there is trauma, you can't just shake it off or get over it. You can manage the pain, ignore the pain, face the pain, but you can't just make it go away. When that trauma leads to Post Traumatic Stress Disorder, the damage may have such an impact that it creates physical changes inside the brain and to brain chemistry, which can change a person's response to future stress. What we know about psychological trauma comes from ERs and war zones, too—the part you can't see and that doesn't always heal on its own.

Pregnancy happens both in the body and in the psyche. Expecting mothers spend a great deal of time preparing for birth. They read books, attend childbirth classes, visit websites, watch TV programs, talk to friends and family, take up yoga, interview care providers, hire doulas, visit hospitals and birth centers. We want to be educated and prepared for the healthiest, want positive outcome for ourselves and our babies. Preparing for birth is sometimes a way of feeling in control of what cannot totally be controlled. There is much written about the current trend to medicalize birth and the escalating rate for cesareans in the U.S., but at the heart of the matter, birth will always have risks. Most natural birth advocates agree that a "good" rate for cesareans in the country would be 10%. It is not ever going to be zero. And even if it were more clear that cesareans were performed only for true crises, there will continue to be trauma. Not all outcomes are what we want to expect. Not all babies are going to be born healthy. Trauma can occur when valiant efforts are taken to save lives. Trauma can occur when the worst outcome you planned to avoid becomes the reality.

There are many situations that can leave you with a story of birth that feels wrong, that hurts like hell to think about, and is not what you expected. It may be a medicated or surgical birth that you sought to avoid. It may be a medical crisis for yourself or your baby that led to overwhelming feelings of powerlessness. It may be being subjected to unacceptable, unethical, or violent actions at the hands of the people to whom you had entrusted yourself. It can be physical pain that is out of control or a bad reaction to a medication or a human error.

It may be difficult to acknowledge that your experience is "bad enough." You may feel that you are making something out of nothing, hanging on to the past, being ridiculous, or simply overreacting. Sadly, this is a very normal part of a traumatic experience because the definition of trauma is a normal reaction to something that is beyond our usual experience. How can you judge what is normal when the situation is so intense? If you find it difficult to talk about all the feelings that you have about your birth, if your birth story doesn't make you happy, if you only share part of your story or gloss over details, this is the book for you.

Some women reading this book may not be able to say, "well at least you have a healthy baby." If you lost a baby at the time of your birth trauma, you may have a hard time reading this book unless you have had time and worked through a great deal of your grief. The women sharing their stories are mostly facing their experience with a positive outcome—the baby is "fine." Some women find it possible to separate their loss issues from their trauma issues and work on them independently, as well as their grief. Take it slow. You may feel that you get a great deal of support and recognition for the loss of the baby, but not for your own trauma. I strongly suggest you find other mothers who have similar losses to connect with, don't go it alone.

Use your best friend voice. People are either their own best friend or their own worst enemy. Seldom do people come into therapy being their own best friend. That voice in your head may be overly critical, unforgiving, harsh, demeaning, or frustrated. When I ask women to listen to each other's birth stories, I ask them to check for their best friend voice. When we listen to other women share their birth trauma, it is natural to bring enormous compassion to our listening. We are certain that they did all that they could do, that of course it wasn't their fault, that they in no way deserved the treatment they received. We believe this with absolutely no evidence except that they seem like lovely women and we can see how much they are hurting. We respond with tenderness. If we bring this energy to our own story, it is much easier to heal. When we are harsh, we keep the wounds open. I ask you to consider that if every other woman deserves your compassion and understanding, then you do as well. As you work through your story, only use your best friend voice with yourself.

If you catch that harsh bitch showing up to rip into you, find a way to break the cycle. It can be very difficult to stop the nastiness alone. If you are in your head, then you need to find a way out. Talk to someone. Write in your journal. Distract yourself. Crank the tunes. Take a look at yourself in the mirror. Anything other than thinking. Thinking can be destructive. It takes a great deal of patience and practice to learn not to use a harsh voice with yourself. Replacing harsh words with positive affirmations can feel uncomfortable and at times downright silly. Isn't it sad that beating yourself up is normal and comforting yourself is weird?

Negative thinking can be like superhighway pathways in your brain. We go there so easily. It is often a knee jerk first response to attack and blame. Somewhere in our brain is a small cow path of positivity, compassion, forgiveness. When you do something stupid or feel like you made a mistake, you end up on the negative path without making a decision to go there. Where you have power to make a choice is the moment that you notice. Finding yourself beating yourself up simply means it is a habit to do it. Breaking the habit is taking one breath and looking for another option. It means pushing back. Choosing compassion over harshness.

Affirmations are a great way to change the normal, habitual response that you have in your head. It takes repeated effort to reprogram yourself to be positive and affirming, especially when you feel you have done something wrong or disappointed someone you care about. A couple of simple affirmations that you might find helpful are listed. Consider putting them on Post-it notes or in your calendar or on your bathroom mirror. It takes time and repetition to get good at being your own best friend, but the benefits are enormous. Try reading them out loud to see how you respond to them.

Mistakes happen.

I deserve to be treated well.

Loving myself heals my life. I nourish my mind, body, and soul.

I release the past.

I give love and it is returned to me multiplied.

I choose to make positive healthy choices for myself.

When I believe in myself, so do others.

I forgive myself.

I express my needs and feelings.

I am my own unique self—special, creative, and wonderful.

Forgiving makes me feel light and free.

It is now safe for me to release all past traumas and move into healing.

I am a forgiving and loving person.

I am at peace.

Life is a joy filled with delightful surprises. I trust in the process of life.

Life is an ongoing lesson. I am still learning.

Most of us are more compassionate with others than we are with ourselves. We are more forgiving, have more patience, and assume that people are doing the best that they can. When you are compassionate with others, look for the similarity to your own situation. Are there mistakes that you think don't get to be forgiven? What are your beliefs about forgiveness and blame? In some families, blame-who did it, whose fault is it- matter a great deal. Is it possible for bad things to happen to nice people? What do you believe about mistakes and human error? Does someone need to pay? Are you vengeful? Are you punitive? You may find it helpful to work on changing your internal dialogue about mistakes and forgiveness. You spend a great deal of time in your own thoughts, in your own head. Shouldn't it be a nice environment? Don't you deserve to be treated respectfully at all times? If people could read your mind, would they be shocked? Would you ever use that tone or that language with someone else?

Another reason to work on this is that being a loving and compassionate mother is a lot easier if you start by being loving and compassionate with yourself. Whatever happened in your birth, it is not the last trauma you are likely to face. It is not the last mistake you will make. Self-acceptance and compassion are like muscles you can build. They are habits that last a lifetime.

This might be a hard book to read. If you have experienced trauma of any kind, it can leave you vulnerable to being emotionally overloaded by things that remind you of that trauma. A trauma trigger is anything that causes a dramatic re-experiencing of a traumatic memory in someone who has experienced trauma. A trigger is a harsh reminder of a traumatic event, although the thing that causes the trigger isn't necessarily frightening or traumatic. Triggers can be almost anything and happen out of nowhere. They can be people, places, noises, images, smells, tastes, emotions, animals, films, scenes within films, dates of the year, tones of voice, body positions, bodily sensations, weather conditions, time factors, or any combination. Triggers can be subtle and difficult to anticipate, and can sometimes make Post Traumatic Stress Disorder, a condition in which trauma survivors cannot control the recurrence of emotional or physical symptoms, or of repressed memory, worse.[1]

Simply picking up this book will be triggering for some women. This is a normal response and not weird at all. It can be painful and it can keep people from the healing work that they want to do. Here is my recommendation. Think about healing trauma work like scuba diving. You go deep into the work and then you can come to the surface slowly. If you start to get overwhelmed, put the book down for a while and take a break. There is no hurry. Do this work at your speed. There is time, you get to control your journey. You might find it impossible to read this book on the bus or at the office. It might be good for bedtime reading because you might find yourself getting very tired and only able to read a few pages a day. Or you might find reading this book makes it hard for you to sleep, respect that feeling and try a bit each

---

[1] Adapted from http://en.wikipedia.org/wiki/Trauma_trigger

morning. It is important to honor the way that you heal. Trust your instincts to want to both resolve your trauma and your instinct to shy away from the pain. Both will work for you on this journey.

I suggest you grab a notebook or journal and keep it handy. Take some notes, highlight things that resonate or upset you. All of your emotional responses to this work are important and valid. I even encourage you to hate some of what I say or to think I'm nuts. (Actually I would love emails telling me those stories. I expect to stir up big feelings and know that not all of them will be the pretty ones.) OK, that said...I welcome you to my book. Addressing trauma is sometimes scary stuff and I give you a lot of credit for stepping into it. At the end of each chapter I will offer a couple of questions for you to write or think about to help you dig deeper.

<u>Digging Deeper</u> Reread the list of affirmations. If you can, read them aloud. Pick two affirmations that appeal to you, that seem like a bit of a stretch for you, and write them in your notebook. Write them in your calendar, write them on your bathroom mirror. Take a moment and think about or write yourself a quick note using your best best friend voice. What would you say to a friend if she were brave enough to work through her birth trauma?

You may work through the exercises in this book in a day, in a weekend, in a month, or over the course of a year. You may pick up this book one time and then forget about it for months. There are some women who will simply read through the information and feel complete with their experience, others will find the exercises very valuable. Some of you will want to talk to lots of other women or go to the Internet looking for other women's birth stories. This is your journey and there is no wrong way to do it. But I will predict that no matter how it goes for you, it won't go exactly the way you expect or the way that you want.

<u>Note to care providers, partners, and family members</u> If you were present and involved with a traumatic birth, you certainly have your own complex feelings about it. If you love someone who had a damaging birth experience and you are worried about them, this topic can be valuable. I appreciate your interest in this work, but didn't write this book with you in mind. I figure that there are over 250,000 women each year who prepare for a natural birth and end up with a negative experience. This is our book. On the other hand, there aren't enough books addressing this topic so I appreciate that people who are concerned about a loved one's birth experience, or are invested in helping other women, will be reading along. It is possible for people who witness a traumatic birth to experience secondary birth trauma, especially if they are deeply connected to the mother. Partners or parents can feel horribly powerless when faced with the fear of losing their loved ones. This book is certainly appropriate for those who have suffered secondary birth trauma. I think many men go into birth poorly prepared for the emotional roller

coaster they are in for. It is the birth of their child. It is their birth story, their experience as well. I will take care to address partner/husband issues as appropriate. When the person you love gives birth, the expectation to be supportive and wonderful is high. I have also heard from many nurses, doulas, and other birth professionals who have experienced birth trauma and need a place to support their work as well. They carry their own expectations and fears into each birth. They care deeply for their patients and empathy is powerful when loss occurs. Be patient and welcome to our journey.

Chapter 2
Why Not Just Get Over It?

A pearl is a beautiful thing that is produced by an injured life. It is the tear [that results] from the injury of the oyster. The treasure of our being in this world is also produced by an injured life. If we had not been wounded, if we had not been injured, then we will not produce the pearl.

-Stephan Hoeller

So, what's the big deal? You knew birth would be painful and you knew there could be complications. So what if you didn't get the birth that you expected? Get over it, right?

Get over it is right. For the vast majority of women who suffer from birth trauma, time will take care. It won't hurt so bad in a year as it does in the first weeks following your birth. You might find that telling the story, "I'm fine, at least the baby is healthy," becomes your mantra and after a while, when you say it again and again and again it might begin to feel as if it is the truth about your experience.

Trauma unresolved does have unwarranted consequences. Whether it's the impact of the rawness in the first few weeks or the long-term wounds that stay tender for years, trauma hangs around. It can be draining. Unresolved trauma increases a woman's risk of postpartum mood disorder. Issues come up in the labor and delivery room that leave a negative impact on her relationship with her family, with her partner, even with her baby. Trauma can leave a woman doubting herself, feeling like a failure, and insecure in her mothering instincts.

You may find yourself wavering between "I'm fine" and "this is the worst thing that ever happened, and I don't know if I will ever be the same." This can fluctuate within the day, even within moments. You are right. You *are* fine. Give yourself a moment to acknowledge all that you are managing well. This hasn't stopped you. Your birth is not the end of the story. Your birth is not who you are. You probably ate breakfast this morning and at some point recently took a bath and responded to the baby and care deeply about being a great mom.

It also can be the worst thing that has ever happened. It can be the horrible thing that reminds you of other horrible experiences. And if birth is transformative, then this journey has changed you, in many complicated ways. The story isn't over yet.

What is Birth Trauma?

Psychology defines a traumatic event as one in which "The person has experienced, witnessed, or was confronted with an event or events that involved actual or threatened death or serious injury, or a threat to the physical integrity of self or others and the person's response involved fear, helplessness, or horror." This definition is from the DSM-IV. DSM is the *Diagnostic and Statistical Manual of Mental Disorders* published by the American Psychiatric Association. It is kind of the dictionary of psychology, it is how we bill insurance and share labels with other professionals.

We live in a culture that has become removed from natural birth. Before a woman goes into birth, it is unlikely that she has ever seen a birth—most of us haven't even witnessed animals giving birth. Our society talks obsessively about fear and risk around childbirth. The risk for trauma is high when we are surround by big emotions, fear of risks, and impossibly high expectations. Intense feelings of fear and helplessness are common in the face of serious medical decisions when both a woman and her baby's life can feel like they're on the line.

Births are not either traumatic or not. Many women have beautiful births in which there was one moment when they were faced with an overwhelming sense of unexpected loss of power. That moment, a week after the birth may simply resolve itself, or it may become an obsessive sore spot that begins to take over the best parts of the story. Even in horrible, terrifying births, there are often wonderful things going on. The nurse who stayed by your side, the thing your partner said that you will never forget, the first moment you saw your baby. These things are also true. Trauma occurs in moments. Birth is a place where women are particularly vulnerable to trauma because of the intense emotional and physical experience. It is also risky because many women today believe that preparing for birth will allow them to remain in control of their birth and protect them from unwanted interventions. Preparing for childbirth must also include awareness of what might happen, what might be hard.

Cheryl Beck, the primary researcher in this area says that, "trauma is in the eye of the beholder;" that trauma is a powerfully personal experience. She has, however, found that trauma is a very complicated mix of objective (e.g., the type of delivery) and subjective (e.g., feelings of loss of control) factors.
Some factors include:

       * Lengthy labor or short and very painful labor
       * Induction
       * Poor pain relief
       * Feelings of loss of control
       * High levels of medical intervention
       * Traumatic or emergency deliveries, e.g., emergency cesarean section
       * Impersonal treatment or problems with the staff attitudes
       * Not being listened to
       * Lack of information or explanation
       * Lack of privacy and dignity
       * Fear for baby's safety
       * Baby's stay in the NICU
       * Poor postnatal care

* Previous trauma (e.g., in childhood, with a previous birth, or domestic violence)

The healing process for the emotional trauma includes working through the memories and feelings associated with the birth. Slowing down and taking time to work through the memories allows the pent up "fight or flight" energy, the automatic responses, to dissipate. Healing your birth trauma means taking space to experience the overwhelming feelings that weren't available during the actual birth. Expressing these big emotions, rather than suppressing or hiding or denying them, is a powerful tool in working through full self-expression of your birth story. Finally, the healing process must work through the sense of betrayal and distrust. Restoring relationships, restoring trust in oneself, in one's ability to make decisions, in one's ability to be cared for and protected when vulnerable is the final step in moving into a positive resolution to your birth story.

One of the reasons that trauma memories are so hard to deal with is that when the event occurred, the thoughts, sensations, and emotions around the event end up stored in different areas of the brain, in a system that is not working cohesively. We can have feelings show up without a thought, we can have sensations that make no sense to us, or we can have pieces of the story totally unavailable to retrieve. A memory that has been processed and fully experienced is cleanly in the past. It is easy to look to your own past and think of something that happened that you never thought you would recover from. At some point, you got your heart broken or someone you loved died, and although you can remember the pain, if it is not a trauma memory—or if you have worked through the trauma—you will be able to visit the memory and the emotions without losing yourself to them. That is the goal of trauma work, to integrate the thoughts and feelings in a way that plants the memory cleanly in the past.

Emotional Intelligence is (somewhat simplistically) the ability to identify, assess, and manage your emotions. If you were raised in a wonderful, healthy, emotionally supportive family, you might have acquired a strong language of emotions, be able to name and express a full range of feelings, and feel comfortable with strong feelings. Most of us have a less than perfect range of emotional expression. When I teach parents how to work with their kids around building emotional intelligence, I like to use the analogy of the big box of crayons, the one with the sharpener that we all wanted to have. If you have a great repertoire of emotions, you have shades of blue and a bunch of greens and you know that lemon-yellow won't work for daffodils. Sadness is different than hurt, is different than frustrated, is different than angry, is different than disheartened. Having a word for the feeling accesses ways to have those feelings honored. It is best to have our feelings without judging them as bad or good, right or wrong. It is important to learn to have a way to express big feelings without hurting ourselves or those we love. As we work through birth trauma and issues around loss, it is likely that you will discover the feelings you are most comfortable with—and those feelings that you do not accept or like or know how to express or doubt your right to feel.

Anger, disappointment, sadness, frustration, shame, loneliness are just a few of the feelings women express around childbirth. Many women who struggle with depression have a hard time processing the complex emotions they experience around loss. Depression is destructive and something you need to resist and fight against. It whispers self-defeating, negative talk in your ear. The wonder of grief is that it also whispers in our ears, but grief carries enormous wisdom and can tell us what we need. Many women will experience a loss at the same time they are dealing with a birth trauma. It can be helpful to separate the experience of grieving the loss of a pregnancy or the death of a baby from the trauma of the birth. Feelings of loss and grief move through time. There are no clear stages of grief. Whatever emotions you are feeling are simply part of your experience. Grief is experienced over time, in its own journey. Experiencing grief and trauma concurrently can muddy the waters of your experience. You may find it helpful to think about unraveling the threads of these distinct experiences as you work through your story.

Integrating your memories with your emotions may require learning new skills, addressing feelings that you have been uncomfortable expressing in the past. The raw spots may be connected to struggles from the past. The disappointments occur on top of a history of disappointments. Feeling trapped, misunderstood, or attacked can leave us powerless at just the moment we wanted to be assertive.

We like to think that our memories are fixed, like photos or videos. We "know" that we remember things just the way that they happened. But for good and for bad, memories are much more fluid than that. Think about opening a document on your computer, taking a quick look at it, and closing it. The question will come up: Save Changes? Your brain works kind of like that. You can open a memory and take a new look at it and save it differently than it was filed before. This allows trauma memories to be processed. A memory that is stressful and raw can be looked at and healed and put away in such a way that is much less problematic. It is important that revisiting the memory be done in a supportive, positive manner.

When women come to my Birth Stories workshop, we heal the stories communally. We share in our processing and work through the pain that we as women carry around birth. When women offer their vulnerability, it brings us closer to them. It has us open and care about them and not judge them. That *best friend listening* that each of us carries with us is needed as we work through our trauma. It doesn't help to open our birth story and then judge it harshly, look for our mistakes, doubt our reactions, and minimize our feelings. Returning to the story needs to be done with our best friend ears, with respect and acceptance and compassion.

As you work through your story, it will also be important to start telling more people. Think about where you feel safest. Find people who can listen to your story with their best friend ears. Start with someone you know has dealt with her own pain. Someone who isn't caught up in feeling bad about your birth. It might not be your mother, who takes it personally and has her own issues with birth. It might not be your partner who knows he let you down and can't get your screams out of his memories of that night. It might not be the midwife who has her own story about what happened. Not at first. Those are other lessons to work on. At first let's just get the story out. The one that is pushing for you to tell it.

There is no truth. There is no right way to do this. It is how you feel, what you remember, how it was for you. It is meaningful and powerful and important.

It is debilitating to run around afraid of your own emotions. Emotions are good and valid and important, but we don't honestly want them ruling our lives. I think emotions are a lot like the weather. It isn't always great to wake up to an overcast, dreary day, but we don't necessarily change our plans because the sun isn't out. We check the weather, dress appropriately, and go about our plans. Emotions are like that. Figure out that you're not in a great mood, figure out how to deal with that, and go to work anyway. It doesn't mean that we ignore the feelings or pretend that they aren't real or beat ourselves up about having those feelings, it is just that feelings don't get to vote about what needs to be done.

When we have trauma, our emotions are louder than our reason, and they show up at unexpected times and inconvenient places. It is hard to ignore emotions screaming in our ear. It is hard to ignore rage or terror or agony. As trauma is resolved, our feelings mellow, but while we work through the memories, they can be loud and immediate and out of control. Since these emotions can be triggered by seemingly disconnected incidents, most people spend most of the day numbing out, afraid to feel anything. People with trauma may use chemicals to do this, drinking or smoking or drugs. Anything rather than actually feeling the raw emotion. Most people numb out daily in television, in Facebook, in food, in shopping. We take little nice boring feelings over real ones. And we choose not to care. We disconnect from our lives and our dreams and the people that we love and the person that we want to be. We become something flat and boring and safe.

The more that we are numb to our feelings and live in a bubble, the more vulnerable we are to moments when they burst out, exploding beyond our control. And those moments send us rushing back to deeper withdrawal. Who wants to lose it in front of people, at work, with their friends? Who wants to look like a crazy person? Better to be "fine."

Take control of your big emotions by giving yourself permission to feel them in safe places with the people you love in your own self-expression. Give yourself time to be rageful and furious and terrified and in agony. Give yourself your emotions so that they can stay fluid and present. Stop resisting your emotions. If emotions are the weather, then put on a coat, grab your umbrella, and go out and get drenched.

Anger expressed moves toward justice. Terror addressed moves toward comfort. Pain addressed can heal and give us new strength, deepen our ability to have compassion for the pain of those around us. We have little power within the darkness of our big feelings, but they cannot move on without our expressing them. Give yourself permission to feel them so that you allow yourself to move to a position of empowerment. No one has ever died from crying. When we act like our tears can destroy us, we forget their power to heal. I double dog dare you to give yourself to the full expression of your own powerful feelings. Go ahead and see just how long you can stay with the raw, pure, honest pain.

Once you take time and begin detangling your feelings from the story of your birth, when you feel the feelings and give them time to mellow, when you move past expression and give your story time to heal, you gain a new perspective on what happened in your birth. When you move past what happened to you, and are no longer at the mercy of your story or your mood, you get to the details of your trauma. It allows you to separate the trees from the forest. This allows you to see the beauty and the joy of your birth. You get to see the details, not painting the whole experience with a broad brush as horrible.

Perhaps there were moments that were amazing. Perhaps there were people who treated you wonderfully and held you tight. There are rough spots that should never have been and there are moments you would never trade. Pull those things apart. Take some time to appreciate the wonder of your birth. Give yourself credit for what you endured and where you triumphed. Feel the joy and the wonder and the power of birth.

Perhaps in the midst of it all, when things were happening quickly and the stakes were high, mistakes were made. Who let you down? Who are you disappointed in? Are you mad at the impatient doctor? Did a nasty nurse overstep her role? Did someone abuse their power or ignore your humanity? It is important to distinguish between a mistake and a violation. It is important to separate your reaction from their behavior. Sometimes a touch is soothing and sometimes it is abuse and sometimes it is a misunderstanding. Give yourself some time to consider that you actually may have been abused and might need to address actions that were violations. Dealing with it might mean asking for an apology, it might mean filing a complaint. If it is a family member or your partner, it is very important to work through your violation with them in order for the relationship to be whole again. If you feel that you made a real mistake, you need to make peace with that mistake and ask yourself for forgiveness.

When we feel betrayed, either by people we love or by our care providers, it has us question our own choices. Who did you pick to be in the room with you?

How did you not know them better? How could you have been so foolish to count on them? Work through the blame and fault finding with your best friend voice. People are less than perfect. You can not control and predict all possible outcomes. If people betray you, it does not mean you were wrong to trust them.

Digging Deeper This is a lot of information. Page back through this chapter and notice what ideas struck you as most helpful in your healing journey. What are the biggest surprises? What ideas make you most uncomfortable? What wounds do you think you are still carrying? Think about something hurtful that has happened in your past. What was important in your healing?

Partners/Family What role can you play in making the person you love feel safer to share her story with you? How do you handle the expression of big feelings? Are you ready to ask her to talk about how you may have let her down? Don't ask if you can't hear it yet. Don't offer to hear her story until you can be her rock.

Chapter 3
Write, Write, and Write Some More

Joy and sorrow are inseparable...together they come, and when one sits alone with you...remember that the other is asleep upon your bed.

-Kahlil Gibran

OK...you need to write your birth story. Enough talk. It is time to get to the work. There are a million reasons not to write. There is no perfect time, no perfect space. There is only put your butt in a chair. Here is the quote I kept on my refrigerator while writing this book: "A writer who waits for ideal conditions under which to work will die without putting a word to paper." -E.B. White. I also needed, "Done is better than perfect."

When you to begin to write your birth story, you need to put words down as quickly as possible. The part of your brain that we are trying to access is creative and powerful and honest. You need to turn off the part of your brain that is your editor or critic. That part of your brain is not helpful right now. The wonderful stuff happens when you give yourself permission to tell your tale. Just get it out, raw and whole. Don't worry about whether it is right or if you are missing something or whether someone would disagree with you. In fact if it helps, consider writing the story that would most piss off your doctor or the evil nurse who just didn't get it or whomever you believe is trying to keep you from your story. Write the story that will make people mad. Write the story that gets the most junk out of your system. Write the story the way it felt. Raw and bloody and wrong and violent and unfair and stupid. Write.

There are many layers to your story that will be helpful for you to write. I suggest you start with the first telling, then answer the questions I offer. Some of them will seem simplistic or irrelevant and some of them will open a can of worms for you. Simply begin pulling back the layers and uncovering what else there is to say about your birth. Language is a powerful tool. It is how we file most of our memories. It is how we make sense of the world and by writing we can find where we have untapped pain and where we have untapped strengths.

In the middle of working on my Healing Birth Stories workshop, I was going along with one of the journaling exercises, probably for the fourth or fifth time, when I hit a raw nerve. In that moment, in a room full of new mommas, paid participants I was struck with a moment of raw panic. I realized that in the over 25 years since Nate was born, I had fiercely avoided general anesthesia. I was terrified of it, avoided it, and on some level hated it, but had no awareness of this. In that moment it was a tiny piece of newly discovered trauma. The thought of a mask being put on my face made my heart race. I remember that when he was two or three, I had to have my wisdom teeth extracted and everyone told me that general was the way to go. I chose to be awake instead. I remember telling people that I was afraid that Nate might need me, that as a single mom I couldn't be away from him that long. Something like that. Now that it is uncovered, I can feel the connection between how I handled that procedure and my trauma. Of course I never wanted to be separated from Nate again. Of course I was afraid that if I was under, somehow I would miss something important. That is precisely what had happened at his birth.

Knowing that I have a raw nerve around general anesthesia is helpful. I haven't had it come up. I suppose if I got hit by a bus, they would just put me out and my having trauma would be the least of my concerns. I do know that if the doctor told me that I needed some kind of surgery and needed to be put out, I would now know what I am up against. I have a clear story and my fear is grounded in reality. Now when I remember, or when anesthesia comes up, I practice breathing and thinking about it. It is kind of like I am taming that memory, just in case I ever need to handle it differently in the future. I don't want my past trauma making decisions about my medical care. I want to be able to make those decisions from a place of strength and certainty. It has been almost 30 years since my trauma and it has been 10 years that I have been consciously addressing it. That doesn't mean that it is gone or that it doesn't have an impact. It is for the most part resolved and I have a lot of control over how I respond to my memories.

42

Journaling Tools, Tips, and Prompts

Journaling works on the brain as a form of meditation and
healing.
Journaling safely releases and explores strong,
uncomfortable feelings.
Journaling provides space for change, new interpretations,
different perspectives.
Journaling slows down the processing of vivid, intense
memories.
Journaling offers privacy and allows for full
self-expression of things that have been difficult to say or
admit to yourself or to others.

If you have successfully used journaling in the past
to handle big emotions, please do whatever works best for
you. One of the best healing tools for trauma is telling the
story, over and over again. This can be done by talking to
someone, but writing it and being able to read it is
powerful. Our brain processes writing and talking
differently, so as we move through the journey to
resolution, try using both as much as possible. Write and
read, write some more, have others read it, read it again,
write some more. This is a fluid, ever-changing story.
If you have never used journaling, here are some quick tips
for getting the most out of your efforts.
Journaling can be done in a plain notebook, a
fancy bound journal, or on your computer. Some people
find writing by hand opens up their emotions more

powerfully and some people find keyboarding much more natural. There isn't a right way, but it is important to pick the way that works for you. I personally buy lots of fancy journals and almost never use them. I find it super intimidating to write on blank white sheets. I do better with yellow legal pads, but I do like fancy colored gel pens that write super fast.

Write freely. Don't worry about spelling or grammar. Cross things out, doodle, draw arrows, or write in the margins. This is for you alone. It doesn't even have to be legible if you are processing hard and fast, just go with it. Don't let sentence structure or paragraphs stop you. Write for yourself, don't worry about who you might hurt or what it might mean. Even if you prefer to use a computer for your journaling, it might be a good idea to carry a small notebook with you because once you open up the wounds from your birth, you may find ideas showing up at unexpected times.

Give yourself time. Try blocking out at least 30 minutes to go into the pain of your story. Try to turn off the phone, get a babysitter, go somewhere private, make a cup of tea or pour a glass of wine, and give yourself permission to go into what you have worked so hard to control and maintain. Bring tissues. If tears come, allow them. Try not to pull back from the pain for at least 30 minutes. Most of us were raised in families that are not comfortable with expressing big feelings. We fear going into the pain, fear we will be unable to come back. That once we start crying, we will never stop. Many of us received the message that crying wasn't OK or that we were being too emotional or that we needed to "get a handle on ourselves." Crying makes other people feel very uncomfortable.

Version #1 — The Big Lie

It can really help you get started on telling your tale if you get the bullshit out of your system first. Purge yourself of the story you have been telling yourself. Write the "No Big Deal" or "I'm Fine" story. Write all the voices that are in the way of your deeper truth. Write what you tell people who you just don't think will understand. Write down every lie you have told, what you told your doctor, your mom, what you tell pregnant friends.

Version #2 — How It Feels

Remember that your memory is fluid, flexible, and changeable. There is a trauma file in your brain that needs to be opened and processed to access your most powerful healing energy. This is the story that you may want to write again and again and again. Make an appointment with yourself to give yourself time and privacy to go deep into the whole memory. Start wherever it makes sense to start. We often have a strong sense of the deep roots our trauma has. There may be things you blame yourself for that occurred long before you even conceived. Let the story begin where it feels like it should begin. Remember that your editor, perfectionist, analytical brain will not be needed for this and can be quite distracting. Imagine that your high school English teacher is over your shoulder and trying to interrupt you. Just tell her to SHUT UP. This is your story and no one is going to stop you from telling it. Now stop reading and go write.

Version #2.1 — Do It Again (and again)

The healing occurs as we write, read, accept, feel what our story is. After you have finished your first full telling of your story, give it some time to mellow. Put it away for a few days. Trust that what you put on paper is powerful and important. When you are ready to go back to your work, approach your story prepared with your best friend voice. Do not edit it. Do not take a pen to it or change a word that you wrote. This is how it was for you. If it doesn't feel the same, or you disagree with something, that is proof that your memory is already unlocking its healing power. Simply read the story and begin to consider writing it again.

Version #3 — Digging Deeper: Going After Sore Spots

It is likely that as you tell your story, you will find some things that will overwhelmed you. There are places in your story that you can't remember or you have a strong sense that you are missing something. There may be pieces of your story that seem confusing or impossible.

46

Remember that by definition, trauma occurs when events are bigger than you are able to process. Your brain has tons of amazing information, but not all of it is stored in ways that make it simple to access. Read through the following list of questions and find the one or two that seem to affect you the most. This can be just what you were thinking or feeling, or they may be the ones that at first glance make you angry or you hate. Just pick a couple and allow yourself to dig into your memory banks looking for answers.

Where does your trauma exist in the physical world? When you drive around town, where are you reminded of your trauma? Are there places you hate to go or places you refuse to go? Are there places that remind you of your trauma? Have you returned to "the scene of the crime"?

When is your trauma? What was the weather like? Do you feel anniversaries approaching? Has it changed how you feel about a time of year or a time of day? Is there a seasonal quality to your loss or pain?

How does your body carry your trauma? Are there physical expressions of it? Do you get headaches or stomachaches or pains that remind you? Are there ways that you sit or ways that you can't be touched that you know are related to your trauma? Are there medical procedures that are much more difficult now?

What are the senses of your trauma? Do you associate smells or tastes with the event? Are there things that you cannot tolerate anymore?

Who is it hardest to consider talking about your trauma with? Does your partner know that you consider your birth traumatic? Would you ever consider talking to your care provider about your anger? Have you talked to your mother, your sisters, your best friend? Who would be most surprised that you are doing this work? Who do you wish would read this book? Who would never get it, even if you told them the whole thing?

Who are you most disappointed with? Who are you most angry with? Who are you most afraid to confront? Who do you most want an apology from?

Are there pieces of your birth that feel almost perfect, beautiful, or spiritual? Which moments seem to be most wonderful? What things surprised you in a great way?

Are there things that you are ashamed of? Are there minutes that you think that if only one thing would have been done differently, everything would have turned out differently? Are there things that you blame yourself for? Are there thoughts that you have not said out loud?

What part does your baby play into your trauma? Are you sorry for what they went through? Do you feel unexplained anger or resentment toward your baby for their experience? Is there a moment where you are angry with yourself for not thinking of them?

Before your birth, you made decisions about your birth, your body, this baby. Do you have regrets? Do you think that somehow this was deserved or expected or connected to your choices?

Are you angry with God? Do you feel that somehow your spiritual beliefs about birth or life or yourself were betrayed in your birth story? Were there moments when you made life decisions in your birth? Did you make promises to yourself or God that you aren't so sure were a good idea?

Partner/Family Write your story of the birth. If you were there, you have your own story. If you weren't there, you also have the story as it unfolded for you. Don't censor yourself. This is just for you for now. Just honor your own truth in this trauma. You have your own fears, worries, moments. The best thing you can do is to get clear with your own truth.

Chapter 4
Resolution—The Journey

Grief should be the instructor of the wise. Sorrow is knowledge: they who know the most must mourn the deepest.

-Lord Byron

If you're going through hell, keep going.
-Winston Churchill

How will I know when I am healed? What should I expect? How does this work? Does it ever go away? When women come into our workshop, one of their biggest needs is for some road map of the healing journey. Needing to predict and control is a natural response to trauma and anxiety. Healing occurs over time with the right support, when we do the work there is to do. Healing slows when we pick at the scab, when we shut down and blame, when we beat ourselves up, or get lost in the guilt. Healing happens, but it is not a linear path. Some days life seems pretty normal and then you watch a Today Show piece about the cesarean rate, or your best friend has a birth that is better than or worse than your birth. We have good days and we have bad. And we don't ever get to have it fully go away. Healing does not mean that the birth becomes something good or that you necessarily feel at peace with your birth. Healing does not mean that you get amnesia.

You know that your healing is going well when you notice that it has been a series of good days in a row. You might find yourself thinking about your birth differently or being able to experience the wonderful pieces of the story. Healing means moving your birth story from the present where it is raw and intense and unpredictable to the past where it is over and complete and perhaps sad, perhaps frustrating. You know that you are on the right path when you stop defining yourself by your story. You become a good mom and a nice person and a compassionate friend who also had a rough birth.

I love to think about healing like those huge skinned knees I used to get as a kid. Wiping out on my bike, I would rip the hell out of the skin and it would bleed and hurt terribly at first. Soon, it would begin to scab over and the pain would become a dull ache. Of course because it was my knee, it often would break open and bleed a bit again, healing and hurting. The first days it hurt all the time and then later it only hurt when I bumped it. After a week or so, the scab would begin to itch and feel tight. Pieces would flake off, or I would pick at it to reveal the pink, soft new skin growing beneath. A month later and it was mostly gone, pink and fresh with just a couple of white longer lasting scars, which would fade over time. It heals. It heals because our cells hold the genetic code for healing. Our job is to keep it clean, try not to bump it open, or pick at the scabs and leave it be. Mostly people heal but sometimes complications arise.

You might have heard about the stages of grief. Elizabeth Kubler-Ross wrote *On Death and Dying* in 1969 and changed the way we think about loss. She laid out stages that people go through when they lose someone that they love. The stages are 1) denial 2) anger 3) bargaining 4) depression 5) acceptance and hope. Perfect. Walk through your steps and you get to acceptance and hope. Just knowing it is possible can make things easier to accept. The book was wonderful. It gave people permission to have a full emotional expression of their loss. It started off only about death, but we quickly learned that all losses are grieved in a similar way. Grief is what we feel when relationships end, when we face infertility, or when our child has a disability. For a lot of people, the main idea that came out of her work was that you often feel angry at people that die and leave us. That seemed weird and wrong before she put it in her book.

The problem that has evolved so many years after she wrote the book is that now people have taken her theory and turned it into something that it was never meant to be. There aren't actually stages. Grief doesn't go from A to B then C in some predictable, one-at-a-time way. The vast majority of people feel like their hearts are broken when they suffer a loss, but they manage to go about their lives as the pain diminishes. The array of emotions of grief can all show up in an hour or a day. Some people will never feel angry and others will spend the vast majority of their time in anger. And that's perfect. Some people feel beat up by the stages, as if they were doing it wrong. There is a rush to get through the stages, as if the only goal was to get through to acceptance and peace. In many ways we have a culture in overdrive, wanting things like healing to happen overnight. There simply isn't an easy fix for healing.

As a therapist, grief is considered normal and healthy and not something to treat unless it is what we call "complicated grief." Complicated grief is kind of funny since I don't know anyone's grief that would be considered simple grief. By psychological definition, complicated grief is grief that gets kind of crazy. Complicated grief has a delusional, lack of contact with reality component. Complicated grief is when you cannot accept reality, when you don't want to know your loved one has died, or you don't remember that you've lost a baby. Don't worry too much about this, it doesn't happen very often. My point is just that no matter how you are doing your grief, you are doing it well. If you are feeling it, that's great. That is healing.

For some of my clients, it can be difficult to separate grief from depression. The heavy sense of sadness can be confusing. Depression whispers in your ear to go back to bed and isolate. It tells you that it has always been like this and it will always be like this. No one understands and no one can help. Depression is seductive. Grief's voice is more comforting, positive, and healthy. It moves you forward and gives you permission to take care of yourself. The risk is that grief can trigger an episode of depression, especially in someone who has a prior history of struggling with depression.

Almost everything I know about surviving grief I learned from my clients. I worked with an amazing family who buried two of their three children after a horrible car accident. I met them for the first time even before they had the funeral. Anna and Matt and their surviving daughter Justine set up an appointment because they believed in the power of therapy, and knew that they were going to need some help. And I knew I had nothing to offer them. What do you say to people who have lost not just one child, but two children?

I learned a lot. I learned you don't say much and you don't try to make it better. That would be disrespectful. When someone you love dies, you don't want to feel better; you shouldn't feel better, not yet at least. On the first day they came to my office, Justine brought her knitting with her. I later learned that she had been knitting obsessively since the day of the accident. She had never really knit before, but she knew somehow that knitting was the "answer." Knitting didn't make her feel better. Knitting didn't make her siblings come back or change her reality. Knitting kept her head from exploding. And so she knit. She knit things that looked like scarves but would never actually "be" anything. She knit because her grief told her to knit.

Listen to your grief. Be open to what your pain is telling you. Do what you know to do. Avoid numbing out. Drugs, alcohol, TV, work, business, food—there are many ways to hide from what you are feeling.

It is important to allow yourself time to heal and be patient with yourself. It is also important to consider that if you are dealing with untreated depression, it might be time to ask for professional help. Processing and addressing your birth trauma should offer some comfort. Knowing that other women have similar reactions or feelings associated with what happened to them should tame the blame and doubt in your head. If you have worked through your birth story and feel stuck with your response, then it might be time to consider getting some outside help. Therapy can be helpful when you are stuck in your own darkness or when life becomes unmanageable. Therapy can be something you give yourself, a way of honoring your extraordinary experience.

Sometimes, once you've done a large share of the work solo, you may find yourself hungering for someone else to talk to about your story. This is also very normal. Healing can move from a very private, internal process to a more social, relational process. You might want to look for websites for survivors, you might seek out groups for mothers. You may find yourself responding differently when someone does share their birth story. Suddenly, after keeping silent, you may desperately want to tell your story to anyone who will listen.

Choosing to take responsibility for your own healing is a courageous and empowering position to take. Many women will decide that time heals all wounds and they will ignore their pain and manage their trauma internally. Perhaps if we had all grown up in very emotionally healthy and supportive families in a society that honored and respected the healing of emotional pains this would work better than it seems to. It isn't wrong, simply a bit naive perhaps. Healing might occur, but we know too many people whose *give it time* ends up being *ignore it and pretend it didn't happen.*

We can look to modern medicine for models of pain management. Lower back pain is epidemic. If you go to your doctor reporting back pain, you may well be given pain medication or muscle relaxants. These help immediately, and may help over time if you actually take it easy and allow yourself time to heal, but many people will choose pain medication so that they can return to their normal activities as quickly as possible. Little will be done to look into the cause of the pain or long-term solutions. For most people, back pain is associated with poor muscle tone, bad posture, and work environments that are hard on our backs. Those things are not addressed when giving pain medication, and time will do nothing except make things worse.

Emotional healing means addressing the cause of the pain so that the situation resolves and you can be stronger in the face of future stress. For many women, they are shocked to discover that the anniversary of their trauma, which is almost always also their child's birthday, is a rocky day. It is a day of mixed blessings. The weather, the seasons, the world around you provide lots of reminders. Everyone wants to celebrate the birth, and of course your baby's first birthday is a wonderful day. It also marks, for better or worse, the end of their infancy. If it has been a rough year, you may feel you missed out on something. If this is your last baby, this is the end of a chapter of your life.

Many women choose to address their childbirth trauma because they are preparing to have another baby. We know that our chance of having a good birth experience is greater if we go into birth emotionally strong. Unresolved trauma increases fear and emotional reactivity, things that aren't helpful for a positive birth experience. I think it is easy to convince yourself that your untreated trauma isn't costing you anything, that it isn't really a big deal, until you find yourself pregnant. Simply being pregnant or thinking about getting pregnant can actually trigger panic in some women. Many women fear getting pregnant again and will obsess about the risk to the point of damaging their relationship. Most women come out of birth trauma committed to never feeling like that again, and the only certain way to avoid birth trauma is to avoid birth.

You may work through the exercises in this book in a day, in a weekend, in a month, or over the course of a year. You may pick up this book one time and then forget about it for months. There are some women who will simply read through the information and feel complete with their experience, others will find the exercises very valuable. Some of you will want to talk to lots of other women or go to the Internet looking for other women's birth stories. This is your journey and there is no wrong way to do it. But I will predict that no matter how it goes for you, it won't go exactly the way you expect or the way that you want.

<u>Digging Deeper</u> What is your history of loss? What things have you had to "get over" in your past? What is your deepest fear about how long this healing journey might take?

<u>Partners/Family</u> It can be hard to hear that the journey may be long. It can often feel like you have lost the person she was before the birth; that the trauma has taken something from you. The birth, the baby, and the trauma get wrapped up together in a great deal of change. Some of it is wonderful, some of it is messy. Be patient and know that great growth often comes from great struggle.

Chapter 5
You Don't Have to Do This Alone

I not only use all the brains that I have, but all I can borrow.

-Woodrow Wilson

I have been a mom for over 30 years, but I have also been a therapist for more than 20. I don't exactly know the difference between me the mom and me the psychologist. I would feel like I was letting you, my reader, down if I didn't check in on how you're doing about now. Obviously this is a book. If you were at my workshop, I would know if you looked shaky or were sobbing and unable to share. A book is not a person and your best friend is not (I assume) a licensed therapist. There are some things that are best served by the pros. If someone you loved was having a heart attack, a book would be a really stupid plan—you'd call 911!

Having a traumatic birth experience can leave a woman debilitated to the point that it is hurting her health, her family, or her relationship with her baby. Trauma can cause enormous stress, interfere with sleep, ramp up emotions, make it difficult to focus at work, and simply make life much more difficult than it needs to be. Some women suffer from Post Traumatic Stress Disorder

(PTSD), the same reaction that rape victims and combat soldiers face. Some women may struggle with Postpartum Mood Disorders, depression or anxiety that would benefit from treatment in support of working through the trauma. There are also ways that we hold our stress in our bodies that can be helped with treatment.

I certainly can't cover all there is to know about mental health issues and postpartum mommas. I hope that as you go over these basic descriptions, you try them on and consider whether it might be time to reach out. A doctor or a counselor can help you figure out what is going on and what course of treatment is best for you. Remember, if you have been struggling for more than a couple of weeks with feelings that feel out of control or are hurting your quality of life, it is time to talk to someone.

Postpartum Mood Disorders—Depression and Anxiety

Many women with birth trauma end up experiencing some degree of depression or anxiety. It can be very hard to internally recognize this because the symptoms of mood disorder are very seductive. It is like having a devil on your shoulder whispering negative beliefs about you that begin to feel very real and very permanent. In my private practice, I joke that it is easy to diagnose postpartum mood disorders because mothers come into my office telling me that they know that they don't have it.

In the average postpartum populations, 15-20% of women experience significant symptoms of depression or anxiety. The research on postpartum mood disorders has found that there are many possible risk factors and causes of postpartum mood disorders. More research is needed to factor out the chicken and egg problem of whether the risk factors of mood disorders increase the risk for trauma or whether the trauma increases the risk of mood disorders or if some women diagnosed with a mood disorder are dealing only with unresolved birth trauma. Most of the symptoms of postpartum depression and postpartum anxiety overlap with what we would consider a normal reaction to trauma:

Feeling sad, depressed, irritable, angry, anxious, or panicky.
Upsetting and intrusive thoughts.
Feeling out of control or like you're "going crazy."
Having a difficult time bonding with your baby or feeling like a bad mother.
Trouble with eating or sleeping.

Postpartum anxiety is extremely common with new moms and even more so when something actually frightening has happened at birth. Mothers of infants have a powerful momma bear instinct. It is healthy to have a strong intuition, concern, awareness of every breath your baby takes. It becomes anxiety when it isn't helpful information. If you think obsessively about your baby's weight or nursing intake or are measuring and counting all the time, it may be anxiety. If you have the pediatrician on speed dial and they have that "oh dear" tone when you call, it may be anxiety. If you have flashes of weird thoughts that could go wrong or are Googling infant illnesses or are afraid you might accidentally hurt the baby, it may be anxiety. Sometimes anxiety just feels like a tightness or general sense that something is wrong.

Postpartum mommas also sometimes have symptoms of Obsessive Compulsive Disorder, a specific form of anxiety where your thoughts get stuck. You may count or wash or question or redo or be unable to sleep because your thoughts are racing. Intrusive thoughts are ones that feel out of control, pressured, painful.

Postpartum depression also comes in a variety of expressions. Some mothers feel sad and overly sensitive. Sometimes the depression feels more like low self-esteem, especially doubting yourself as a mother or a wife. Often moms have told me of feeling that their families would be better off without them. The depression can be a flat, unfeeling disconnect. It can be irritability or anger sometimes directed toward the baby, older siblings, or your partner.

Postpartum mood disorder is a stupid name because lots of women begin experiencing what is more accurately described as perinatal mood disorders during their pregnancy. Some women I have worked with have felt that their anxiety or depression during their pregnancy greatly increased their risk for birth trauma.

Having a previous history of depression or anxiety, a history of abuse, or strong hormonal mood swings increase your risk of having a tough postpartum transition. It can also run in families. Check with your mom or sisters about their experience. Your risk is higher if your partner is struggling with becoming a parent or has their own mental health issues. Social isolation, lack of support, parenting multiples, high risk pregnancy, bed rest, or health issues with the newborn can also make things harder.

If you have intrusive thoughts that are scaring you, thoughts that seem dangerous to yourself or your baby, please call immediately for help. Postpartum depression is a horrible, but very treatable disease. Part of the problem is that when you are anxious or depressed, it can feel like nothing will help, no one will understand, and that people will think you are a bad mother. Guilt over the thoughts that you are having or the feelings you have simply make it worse. Asking for help takes a great deal of courage, but is the best way to move forward.

Post Traumatic Stress Disorder—PTSD

Some women respond to their trauma in a way that psychologists label Post Traumatic Stress Disorder (PTSD). This reaction was first studied in combat soldiers and was then used to describe the reactions of rape and domestic abuse victims. It is a normal response that some people have to trauma. It is a NORMAL response. It is like your leg breaking or getting a concussion in a car accident.-something assaulted you and your brain suffers the impact of that assault. It is related to brain chemistry and some people appear to have a higher genetic predisposition to PTSD. It is not necessarily a measure of how bad the trauma is. In PTSD, the trauma is re-experienced with intense fear, helplessness, and horror. You may experience intrusive and distressing memories or what we call flashbacks—smells or images or sounds that feel current, not in the past. You may have nightmares that feel like the event is occurring again. The level of distress can be triggered by any cue both internally and in your world that brings up the birth trauma. People who are experiencing PTSD often go out of their way to avoid the things that they associate with their trauma, or avoid things that remind them of the event. To officially qualify for a diagnosis of PTSD, these reactions must last for at least a month and be disruptive to your functioning. It is also common for people dealing with intense trauma reactions to lose pieces of their memory and have a hard time recalling details of the event.

When dealing with this much pain, it may become clear that you have lost interest in all outside activities, especially those that used to make you feel good. You may feel detached, estranged, or disconnected from people you don't believe can understand your experience. It may leave you feeling numb or zoned out or flat, and you may have a sense of doom and hopelessness about the future. Another piece of this reaction is that you get an intense and persistent sense of arousal. Part of your emotional world is shut down and the other pieces may feel out of control. This makes it hard to fall asleep or stay asleep, you may be very irritable or angry at times, you may have a hard time concentrating, or jump easily and startle because you are always on the lookout for something else bad to happen.

PTSD occurs when something happens that feels like it is life threatening, dangerous or threatening to yourself or others, and you experienced the event with intense feelings of fear, helplessness, or horror. Then there is intrusive recollection. These can be memories, dreams, feelings, or triggers. They are usually memories that you do not feel you have control over, and the memories just show up and kick you in the butt. Because these memories feel out of control and painful, most people make complicated efforts to avoid having the memories triggered. For birth trauma this looks like not wanting to talk about birth, yours or others. It might mean turning the channel or avoiding shows about birth. It can be not wanting to go near the hospital or the doctor's office. It might be that certain smells are off limits. Some women find disinfectant or other smells associated with hospitals dangerous, but it can also be the essential oils your midwife was using or your partner's aftershave or the smell of the lotion you had always loved. Just as the smell of cinnamon can send you right back to Grandma's kitchen, the smell of lavender might bring up panic. Some women carry the memory in their bodies and find certain positions or places on their bodies to be triggers. After having a great sexual relationship with your partner, you might suddenly be uncomfortable when he touches your inner thigh or you might jump if you feel like he is restraining your arms. Anything that you do to try and avoid remembering or being triggered is avoidance.

Cheryl Beck observed: "Mothers with Post Traumatic Stress Disorder attributable to childbirth struggle to survive each day while battling terrifying nightmares and flashbacks of the birth, anger, anxiety, depression, and painful isolation from the world of motherhood." In the middle of a traumatic event, a person often does not have time to actually have the natural strong emotional reactions that they are feeling. These feelings get cut off from the memory of the event and end up showing up afterwards as "hyperarousal" or emotions that seem incongruent or out of proportion. Hyperarousal can lead to sleep problems, anger outbursts or irritability, difficulty concentrating, and hypervigilance, which is sensitivity to threats, quick startle response, and intense worry. Hyperarousal is often exhausting and highly stressful.

PTSD is complicated and women who experience PTSD are often doing all they can to just get through parenting without becoming overwhelmed or falling apart. If you suspect PTSD, I strongly encourage you to ask someone to help you locate someone who is well trained in working with PTSD. You deserve to feel better, you deserve support.

Relationship Struggles

The early parenting years are hard on marriage. Two individuals from very different backgrounds come together and begin to form a new family. Issues of loyalty, baggage from our own childhood, terrifying dependence, and loss of identity make the first 12 months one hell of a ride. Add the fact that moms are hormonal and exhausted and in love with the new baby and have extraordinary expectations for themselves and their babies. The marriage often feels a huge impact of that stress. Partners/dads also have their own complicated journey as new parents. They can often face debilitating concerns about being responsible, providing, finding their own way, figuring out how to support their partner, and societal messages of their irrelevance and inadequacy. That is all without birth trauma. Your relationship is precious and investing in it is one of the best things you can do for your emotional well being and for your child's future.

Options for Getting Help

Psychotherapy. Working with a therapist who is experienced in perinatal mood disorders is a great option. This person might be a Licensed Counselor or Psychologist or Social Worker or Licensed Marriage and Family Therapist. You can look for this specialty through resources such as PSI (Postpartum Support International-www.postpartum.com). You can call your insurance and ask them for a referral to someone in your area. Most good therapists should have information on their website about their philosophy, style, and background. Feel free to call and speak to them before your first session. It is perfectly acceptable to interview them and ask them questions before you entrust them with your story. It is also a great idea to change therapists if after 2-3 sessions you do not feel that there is a good connection or that it hasn't been helpful. Never let a therapist make you feel like it is your issue that therapy isn't working. Some therapists who specialize in working with trauma are trained to do EMDR (Eye Movement Desensitization and Reprocessing). This is a special therapeutic procedure that uses eye movements, tones, or taps to reprocess past memories or triggers.

I have some very strong professional bias when it comes to couples counseling. Sadly, lots of really great individual therapists are horrible couples therapists. Couples work is a very specific skill and a good couples therapist will not sit there and let you have the same ineffective conversation (fight) you were having at home. Just ask what special training they have in marriage work; narrative therapy, Emotionally Focused therapy, and system family therapy are some of the secret code words to look for.

Medication. Medication is an option for treating depression, anxiety, sleep disturbances, or PTSD. This may be for a short time, while you get some therapy and begin to regain your strength, or you may need it for some extended period in order to continue to handle the stress of your life. It is possible to get medication through your midwife or family doctor, and many people only use a psychiatrist if they hit complications. A psychiatrist is a medical doctor specially trained in the treatment of mental health issues. If you are working with a psychiatrist or taking medication, it is important to also work with a therapist of some kind. Psychiatrists seldom have the kind of time that you will need to talk about the issues you are working through, and often only see you monthly or every six weeks.

Alternative or Complementary Health Care. It is beyond the scope of this book to go into all the wonderful options for getting support in your healing journey. There are many great options to assist you in your healing. You may find massage, chiropractic, craniosacral therapy, or other body modalities very good at working through trauma that is carried in your body. I have heard great things about Maya Abdominal Massage, particularly for women who have had surgical births. You may also find it very supportive to have healing work from a herbalist, homeopathic medicine specialist, or a Chinese Medicine specialist. Working through your trauma requires a great deal of support and positive energy. Be careful to surround yourself with people whom you trust, who you feel are committed to your healing.

Groups. There are places where women are gathering to support each other through birth trauma work. ICAN, International Cesarean Awareness Network (ICAN-online.org), has been the most supportive agency that I have worked with in this area. They have a wonderful Facebook page both nationally and for local branches. PATTCh (pattch.org) is a new nonprofit group—Prevention and Treatment of Traumatic Childbirth. There are certainly other small community groups doing this work. I believe that finding like-minded women who share your experience can offer very powerful healing support. Check the local parenting agencies, birth centers, and hospitals for places that offer postpartum groups or new mommy groups.

<u>Digging Deeper</u> Take a minute and check in with how you are managing. Are you sleeping OK? Are you eating normally? Do your moods rule your day? Are you having any thoughts that worry you? Are you having flashbacks? This is important work, but it doesn't have to be done alone. Who have you talked to about your birth? Have you let your midwife or doctor or your baby's doctor know? Is anyone in your family expressing concern about how you are doing? Have you talked to your partner about how you are feeling? There are lots of wonderful people out there willing to help. You would tell your best friend that it's a good idea to get some help. www.postpartum.com 1-800-944-4PPD

<u>Partners/Family</u> Having big, complicated feelings about birth is to be expected when there is trauma. Respect your partner's right to have those feeling. However, if you have concerns about her broader emotional state or mental

health, please encourage her to talk to someone. When people are overwhelmed with their mood, they often need help finding help, making those simple phone calls, and reaching out. Make a phone call. Often the easiest person to call first is the provider that delivered the baby. Even if they can't help, they should be able to work with you on finding a provider. Mental health emergencies should be handled as all medical crises, call 911 if you are worried about someone's safety.

Chapter 6
Trauma on Top of Trauma

So often survivors have had their experiences denied, trivialized, or distorted. Writing is an important avenue for healing because it gives you the opportunity to define your own reality. You can say: This did happen to me. It was that bad. It was the fault and responsibility of the adult. I was—and am—innocent.

-Ellen Bass
The Courage to Heal: A Guide for Women Survivors of Child Sexual Abuse

Your birth story is one chapter in your life. It connects to the losses and traumas that you have experienced earlier in your life. Women who have a history of previous trauma are at increased risk to suffer trauma in birth. The most common forms of trauma that young women face are sexual abuse, rape, and domestic violence. Being touched in her genitals, being held down, being betrayed by someone in a position of trust, being powerless, and having her needs and concerns ignored are high risk factors for re-triggering past reactions.

Birth requires us to be in touch with our bodies, accept enormous vulnerability, assert our needs powerfully, and build trusting, healthy relationships with our care providers. These are complicated tasks. Even if you have no history of previous trauma, it is likely that at least one of these was a challenge as you prepared for your birth. Sadly, many women go into birth with a history of previous trauma. The vast majority with a history of abuse were abused by someone that they loved, someone that they trusted, and someone who had power over them. Abuse is a betrayal of trust and makes us respond to the world protectively and defensively.

Normal birth occurrences may be a trigger for women who have a history of past abuse. Physical abuse, sexual abuse, and emotional abuse can damage your sense of wholeness, your self-esteem, and your power. It can leave long-term wounds or sensitivities that come up during birth. If you have been physically abused, your body may struggle relaxing or you may respond strongly to any sense of being restrained or limits imposed on your physical freedom. Something as simple as denying a woman food during her labor can trigger powerful reactions in a woman who has been punished harshly in childhood by being denied food. If you have been emotionally abused, the high tension of a tough birth may have you feeling as though you are being yelled at or manipulated or judged harshly. A history of sexual abuse certainly has complicated implications for pregnancy and childbirth. So much of sexual abuse makes us feel ashamed of our bodies and our sexuality. I remember being so surprised how many people teased me about, "I know what you've been doing," when I was first pregnant—as if my

73

belly was evidence of sexual activity that everyone else got away with. I felt exposed. I felt naked. My breasts growing was a reminder of my awkward early adolescence. I was thrilled that they were an expression of my body changing for the baby, but I also felt uncomfortable about my body again. For many women, going to the gynecologist for a yearly exam is more than uncomfortable, it feels threatening. To have to look forward to this happening with increasing frequency during pregnancy can be very stressful.

It is expected that women birth with their partners in the room and often with a number of other strangers coming and going without notice. Being exposed, naked both physically and emotionally, when you have little control is terrifying. One woman who had been made to be quiet during her rape struggled with not wanting to make noise during her birth, but also wanted the freedom to express herself however she needed to. It was helpful that she was able to identify this concern before her birth and discuss it with the people who would be in the room so that they could attend to this trigger with her. Another woman I know knew that she could manage just about anything but being restrained. When it came time for her surgical birth, she needed a great deal of support to allow her arm to be restrained. But by taking control of this process and talking to her care providers through the process, she was able to experience her arm being restrained not as an act of abuse, but as something she was in charge of.

Many women who are abused, especially if this abuse occurred early in their lives, have learned to disassociate or go out of themselves under stressful circumstances. Dissociation is that weird feeling you get driving down the road when you somehow have traveled miles without really being engaged or thinking about it. You just kind of go into autopilot. It can be a simple thing we do when our mind is bored or lacks stimulation, but it is also a survival strategy for children who have no power to control an abusive situation. If you are unable to get yourself physically safe, there is a way to step emotionally out of the worst of it. This disassociation survival skill can be so powerful and automatic that many women have a difficult time staying present when situations become out of control. During birth, some women go so deep into their own psyches that they do not recall large chunks of time or important events.

Childhood physical or sexual abuse, prior domestic abuse, or rape are enormously relevant to working through your birth story. There are other traumas or prior experiences that can also trigger traumatic reactions. Perhaps you have been injured or in an accident. Perhaps you were sick as a kid and endured extensive intrusive medical procedures. Sometimes prior losses can be mixing in with your birth story, perhaps a death or a major life disruption. Even what we consider secondary trauma—things that have happened to the people we love. Perhaps a friend lost a baby or your sister nearly died in

75

the hospital. All of these are layers of the onion when it comes to your personal trauma experience.

Having a history of trauma increases vulnerability to stress. Trauma can distort our thinking both about the event and about ourselves, our situation, and those around us. When working through your birth trauma, be aware of other incidents in your past and how they may impact or distort your thinking.

Birth Under the Microscope. When we process our birth trauma, we often magnify the negative details and miss many of the positive ones. Often trauma is related to very small details that our focus locks onto and this colors the rest of the story. We pull that detail out of context, isolated from the neutral or positive details, experiencing them louder, more intensely, and more horribly than they may in fact be. Working through those tough moments opens up for recognizing the full experience.

Polarized Thinking. When pushed into a corner, we often experience things in either black or white, good or bad. We only get the extremes of our experience and lose sight of any grey areas of our memory. The greatest danger in having polarized thinking is when we turn it on ourselves and judge our own actions during the birth. We are either perfect or a failure, we are either innocent or at fault. Some reality checking in our certainty can give us forgiveness and peace of mind.

Overgeneralization. When something horrible happens to us, we are inclined to leap to huge conclusions about broader contexts based on a single incident. If something bad happens, we expect it to happen again and again. We experience it as always happening, having always been true, or being just how the world is. This can lead to a highly restricted life by withdrawing from anything that falls inside of our overgeneralized experience. Many women refuse to attempt a natural birth, believing that they could never handle it. Some women even refuse to consider having kids out of their trauma. Or they may decide that no doctor is trustworthy and spend years resisting medical recommendations.

Mind Reading. In the midst of a traumatic event we make huge leaps of judgement, feeling like we know how people are feeling, we know what they are thinking, and are certain about why they act in the way that they do. Specifically, we are certain about their thoughts and feelings about us. We imagine that people feel and react in ways that relate to how we feel. Therefore, in times of trauma, when our emotions are very high, we assume that others are also experiencing big emotions: fear, anger, hatred, impatience, panic. We jump to conclusions and then proceed without any verification of our reliability. I hear this most often when women talk about their partner's experience of their birth and their assumptions about how their partner is judging, frustrated, or blaming them. Mind reading keeps people from listening to each other's true experience.

Catastrophizing. When things get intense, we begin to expect disaster. We notice and hear problems and begin to ask "what if" questions about what could happen to us. We walk ourselves out on the worst ledge, dealing with a perceived worst case scenario. This is based on our concerns about trusting ourselves and our capacity to manage intensity and the unknown.

Personalization. When faced with enormous emotional stress, of course we feel like it is all about us; that everything that is going on around us is related to our own experience. We believe that every reaction that people have is about us. This also leads us to compare ourselves, question our worth, test our value with the people we are in contact with. We want to know that they think well of us, that they think we're doing the right thing. This of course leads to a great deal of self-doubt and insecurity.

Control Fallacies. When going through a traumatic birth, we can distort our sense of power in two distinct directions. We can feel that we have no control, that we are total victims of our situation or we can have the distortion in the other direction in that we are totally responsible for all the pain and impact of all that happens around us. Feeling like a victim leaves us without options for transforming our story. It keeps us stuck. We had no power in the traumatic situation, therefore we have no power to change our feelings about what happened. On the other hand, if we focus on the idea that we had control of the situation and therefore are responsible for everything that was done, we can become exhausted and unable to see the impact that others had in the situation. We fail to hold others accountable when we accept responsibility for choices that we didn't have, decisions that we didn't agree to, or things that happened when we, in fact, had no control.

Fallacy of Fairness. It is easy to get caught in some sense that we are certain that we know how life should be, how situations must be handled and we believe that our sense of what is right is based clearly on our sense of justice and fairness. We forget that there are other people's needs and concerns that we are unaware of, things going on that we do not totally understand. We get caught in stand-off disagreements over someone else's sense of justice and righteousness.

Blaming. We have a hard time not blaming someone when horrible things happen. We can flip between a sense of it either being our fault, which makes us very uncomfortable or if it isn't our fault, then we go in search of someone or something else to blame. It is difficult to imagine that bad things can happen without someone being held responsible. It can be easier to blame larger systems than people that we care about.

Shoulds. Most women go into birth with very clear expectations about how their birth should be. These are not wishes or ideas, but ironclad rules about what kind of birth they deserve. It is easy to convince yourself that if you prepare and exercise and eat right and read the right books then you should be guaranteed a "good" birth. We have rules and expectations—that we may not even be aware of—about how our partner should respond, about how our caregivers should respond, what they should believe. We can become very angry and frustrated when we come up against people who break these rules. In our head, these shoulds are indisputable and judging others or finding fault naturally follow when shoulds go wrong.

Emotional Reasoning. It is often hard to question the reliability of our emotions. Validating our feelings means that somehow they must be warranted. Therefore, if we feel angry, then we must have been wronged in some way and if we feel guilty, then we must have done something bad. If we are sad, then we have suffered a loss. If we are terrified, then something bad must be approaching. It is hard not to feel weak or powerless or abused or misunderstood in the midst of the chaos that can surround birth struggles. The problem is that for the most part, our feeling follows and interacts with our thinking so that if we are dealing with distorted thinking, then we of course will end up with distorted and unreliable emotions.

Being Right. We feel continually on trial proving that our opinions and actions are correct. Being wrong is unthinkable and we will go to any lengths to demonstrate our rightness. Having to be "right" often makes us hard of hearing. We aren't interested in the possibility of a differing opinion, only in defending our own. In birth we have a horrible fear of being wrong about anything that we did or believed.

Heaven's Reward Fallacy. We expect being good and doing the right thing will pay off as if there were someone keeping score. We feel bitter when things don't happened as expected. The problem is that while we are always doing the "right thing," we still cannot prevent bad things from happening. We then somehow feel that if a bad thing happens, perhaps we actually did deserve it. (McKay, Davis, & Fanning. New Harbinger, 1981.). These styles of thinking (or cognitive distortions) were gleaned from the work of several authors, including Albert Ellis, Aaron Beck, and David Burns, among others.

Triggers, from past abuse or from a traumatic birth, are often connected with a pent-up panic response. It is as if we are steeling ourselves to ensure nothing bad ever gets us again. Wikipedia says that "hypervigilance is an enhanced state of sensory sensitivity accompanied by an exaggerated intensity of behaviors whose purpose is to detect threats. Hypervigilance is also accompanied by a state of increased anxiety which can cause exhaustion. Other symptoms include: abnormally increased arousal, a high responsiveness to stimuli, and a constant scanning of the environment for threats."

Trauma occurs when we are trapped in an experience. Most of us would have done anything we could have to get out of the situation. It wasn't something we picked. We got stuck with it. We were powerless in the moment. As humans, we can handle an awful lot if we have control of it, but we hate feeling trapped. Trapped gives us very few psychological options. We can fight. We can roar and scream and strike out. Backed into a corner, we want to defend ourselves. If fighting isn't the best idea, we prepare to run. We want out. We want to hide and get away from the thing that is attacking us. Both fight and flight responses are neurological reactions. Adrenalin shoots into our bloodstream. Stomach acid dumps into our stomach to burn fuel fast for our battle. Our eyes dilate, our pulse races, the blood pulls to our core organs and leaves our hands and feet cold. This fight or flight response is wonderful if a wild animal is attacking...it is not helpful during birth. Depending where and how you birthed, you may have had restrictions on your movements or positions, you may have felt silenced in your vocal expression, you may have been immobilized by tubes or medications, or your choices may have been taken from you with threats of harm to yourself or the baby.

Most of us did not get a chance to run or fight in the midst of our traumatic situation. When that reaction hits and it cannot go anywhere, we end up numbing out. Some people actually disassociate in times of trauma. Dissociation is usually that feeling that you are detached from your body, emotions, or surroundings. Dissociation compartmentalized your experience. You break things into pieces; your conscious experience, your senses, your emotions, and the memory aren't working well together. People who were abused in the past often have learned to use dissociation to handle difficult situations and may dissociate easily. Rape victims talk about leaving their bodies and going to somewhere safe in the midst of their attack. Some pain management increases the sense of dissociation from the experience. We want to be able to separate from the pain, but then we separate from our body, our power, our experience.

After a trauma situation, that feeling of panic or being trapped can hang around for a long time. It leaves you reactive, jumpy, worried, as if there was a war you were ready to fight. It is like constantly living on the edge. It is exhausting. It is hard to trust people. It is nearly impossible to relax. It is important to address the unresolved fears so that the panic can dissipate. The best way to do this is to connect the dots—draw the connections between the feelings that you are having, the fear, the panic, the worries, the jumpiness to the actual source of those feelings. There is nothing wrong with feeling panic. It is a normal reaction to a horrendous experience. Most of us when feeling anxious simply dismiss those feelings. People will tell us that everything is fine, there's nothing to be afraid of, it's nothing. And although that may be true in the moment, there are real things to fear. The fear and jumpiness when you feel constrained by a simple blood draw may actually connect to the moment you were strapped down and sedated, fearing that something was wrong with you baby.

Connecting the dots allows that energy to be released. Think about the moments that make you the most anxious. Is it a place, a situation, a person, a physical sensation? Now how does that make sense? Where does it connect to the moment when terror was appropriate? Can you give yourself permission to accept the panic and feel it? Resisting panic only increases it, as if our subconscious gets louder, the more we try to shut it up. It is important to believe that the intense feelings that you are experiencing

83

do make sense, they simply are disconnected from the thing you are most afraid of, the thing that really is terrifying.

Another very natural response women may have is to numb those feelings. They may disconnect from the memories and the situation emotionally. We may actually not remember huge pieces of the occurrence, or we might not be able to access any emotional response to our own story. When we deaden our response to something, it often has us feeling flat or distant. It takes a great deal of emotional energy to *not* feel what we are afraid to feel. People who respond this way to trauma can even end up feeling that their life isn't important or have an impending sense of doom or failure.

In the middle of a traumatic event, a person often does not have time to actually have the natural strong emotional reactions that they are feeling. These feelings get cut off from the memory of the event and end up showing up afterwards as "hyperarousal" or emotions that seem incongruent or out of proportion. Hyperarousal can lead to sleep problems, anger outbursts or irritability, difficulty concentrating, and hypervigilance which is sensitivity to threats, quick startle response and intense worry. Hyperarousal is often exhausting and highly stressful.

It can be painful to begin to unravel the impact of past abuse on your birth experience. It can bring up complicated issues around blame and responsibility. It will often unlock old rage. Be gentle with yourself and take this slow. The point of considering past abuse, traumas, or losses when re-writing your birth story is to aid the healing process. Being able to identify deep connections and the impact of the past are paths to how life begins to get better.

<u>Digging Deeper</u> This is tough stuff and you might need a break or some support dealing with how your birth relates to any past trauma. Make a list of the big feelings and reactions you have about your birth and see where else in your life these feelings have come up. Make a list of what has helped you resolve past trauma and what healing has felt like for you.

<u>Partners/Family</u> What is your history of trauma? What issues from your past are connected to your feelings about trauma and healing? What part of this chapter were hardest to read? Why?

Chapter 7
Facing Your Rage

We must learn how to explode! Any disease is healthier than the one provoked by a hoarded rage.
                                    -Emil Cioran

Bitterness is like cancer. It eats upon the host. But anger is like fire. It burns it all clean.
                                    -Maya Angelou

        You are either pissed off about your birth or you should be. Anger is a healthy, natural response to threats and attacks, injustice and disappointment. Seems like those things have a lot to do with having your birth go wrong.

        Women have been socialized to swallow their anger, not express it. Too often we were cautioned not to hurt anyone's feelings or not to make a big deal about our own needs. We are often uncomfortable being angry even if we don't express it. We feel guilty for even feeling angry. Recent studies of women's anger show that the three things we get most angry about are feeling powerless, injustice, and other people's irresponsibility. Women, compared to men, tend to stay angry longer, feel more resentful, and are less likely to express their anger. When anger doesn't find its voice, women are at risk for anxiety, stress, and panic attacks. Part of working through your birth story is facing your anger and finding a healthy way to express it.

A healthy anger response should protect us from getting hurt again. Like yelling ouch when someone steps on your foot, expressing your anger lets the people around us know that we are hurt, that we feel threatened. People that are trustworthy will make every effort not to hurt us again. Anger expressed and acknowledged has served its purpose. In good relationships, we shouldn't need to hang on to our anger.

Many of us have past experiences that make it feel risky to express our anger. Perhaps your family told you that it wasn't that big of a deal when you were hurt. Maybe someone in your life took the vulnerability you shared and used it against you. Sometimes expressing anger simply wasn't responded to; didn't buy you any safety or responsiveness. When this happens, you have two choices: hide your anger in order to protect yourself or hang fiercely onto the anger, wear it like an armor to protect you at all times. Resentment chokes us on unspoken hurts. And some people swing back and forth, swallowing and biting back the anger until they blow.

When you look at the anger you have around your birth story, it can be helpful to look at how you have handled issues where you felt threatened in your past. How do you express anger at your partner? Your family? Do you stand up for yourself when someone takes advantage of you? How do you handle injustice?

There is a place where all of us are seven years old

and we want the world to always be fair and make sense and we want to know that when bad things happen, that either it was deserved or that at least we can identify the person to blame. We want to know whose fault it is. We want answers to be simple and our reactions to be pure. In our search for meaning, we bounce around our birth story looking for likely bad guys. I have yet to meet a woman who does not find multiple ways to blame herself for her birth trauma. We want to believe that we were in control, we made choices, and we received an outcome directly related to this. It just isn't that simple.

The pain of taking responsibility for causing your own and your baby's birth trauma is unbearable, so it can ping pong back to finding someone else to blame. We blame our doctors, our other care providers for the things we felt we didn't get to choose. We blame our partners and our family members for their lack of support. We rage against God and the Universe for the injustice. We rage against women who birth easily. We rage against our baby for being "fine" when we are not. The anger feels like it needs a release, someone to absorb the pain.

The first thing we need to admit is that we want it to be someone's fault. We want birth to be sane and predictable and clean. That would make it all so much easier.

If it is our fault, then the outcome is fair. We got what we deserved. If only we would have done the "right" thing, we could have avoided the birth trauma. Because the trauma is so horrible, the next likely truth is that the mistake we made must have been equally horrible. Of course it is possible, in fact likely, that mistakes were made in your birth and that some of those decisions or actions were your mistakes. Or that you made decisions that you can now see you wish you would have made differently. This Monday morning quarterbacking—second guessing decisions that obviously did not work out as planned—makes things look more controllable. We would rather believe that right choices always lead to right outcomes, than face the tough truth that sometimes things go the way they go, no matter what we do.

Birth is at times dangerous. Birth is at times out of control. Life has so many variables that it is impossible to simultaneously prepare for all possible outcomes. We play a messy game of best possible choices with less than total awareness.

Many women who have shared their birth stories with me believe that if only they would have read the chapters about surgical birth and prepared better for the chance of a cesarean, they might have been better prepared, might have understood the risks, and in some way might actually have avoided the surgery altogether. I know just as many women who believe that if they had not considered surgical birth, if they had skipped reading those chapters, and had been more committed to not thinking about negative outcomes, that they would have been better prepared and avoided the trauma and in some way might have actually avoided the surgery altogether. This is called superstitious thinking. It is how we silly humans have come to avoid black cats, ladders, the number 13, and the cracks in the sidewalk. It seems like bad things happen because of something that we do and if only we avoid these "bad luck" things, we can avoid the bad outcomes. We like to put things together that have nothing to do with each other. Now of course reading a book about birth, the thoughts and attitudes that we bring into birth are important. It just isn't the same thing as saying that reading or not reading a chapter is the "reason" that our trauma occurred. There are just too many variables involved. Believe me, if we knew that reading (or not reading) the surgical birth chapter was the way to avoid trauma, even the OBs would be recommending it. It isn't simple. It isn't direct.

Expressing your anger in a healthy way doesn't have to be destructive or aggressive. Assertiveness is taking responsibility for your own feelings. You don't have to justify why you are angry or blame someone else for your feelings. Assertiveness is simply expressing the thing that you feel needs to be expressed. "I statements," like affirmations, have become the thing of comedy routines but they have a real place in good communication.

I felt ____ when you ____. It would help if you ____. When having rough conversations with people that you do not want to alienate, keep it pretty specific and short with a soft lead in, and a focus on the value of the relationship.

Example: *I want to tell you something because (I love you, I want you to understand how I feel, I want to make sure you know that what you did impacted me, I want to be able to move past what happened).*

I felt (hurt, disappointed, pissed off, angry) when you (short and sweet specific action if possible, said what you did, didn't listen to my request, went against your word). It would help if you (apologized, took responsibility for your behavior, didn't make promises you can't keep, spoke to me respectfully).

I appreciate you listening and hope you can appreciate how hard this was for me to tell you.

In assertive communication, we are giving the listener a gift; revealing something important to them. It isn't really a conversation. If they try to argue or defend, it can help to simply stop and ask if they are willing to give you a minute and just listen. Your communication, your feelings aren't up for discussion—they simply are what they are. Defensiveness is a natural response to feeling attacked, and it is natural for many people to take a defensive stance when presented with someone's anger. The point of offering your feelings to them is so that they have a better understanding about how you feel. They might not be open to hearing it, and it is up to you to decide if it is worth the risk to share.

Sometimes it isn't safe or practical to share your feelings with someone. It might be important to you to talk to your doctor, or you might not feel invested enough in taking on that conversation. It might be that you want to talk to your mother about how things went, but just aren't feeling that the time is right yet. You might want to tell your doula that she hurt your feelings, but feel that you are too angry yet to have that conversation. Deciding to have the courage to share your anger in a healthy way with someone is always a risk, and it is your choice how and when to do that.

There are lots of great healthy ways to express anger even if you decide not to deal with the anger directly.

Vent—Tell someone, anyone who will listen and not try and shut you down or argue. Just ask someone to give you time to talk about how angry, hurt, frustrated you are.

Scream—Find a safe place to let it all out. Swear, scream, cry, say some really mean shit. This works great in the car on the freeway.

Write a letter—Write it all down. Write the doctor or the hospital or your doula or your partner. Write to God. Just write down all you want to say. Send it or don't. Burn it or rip it to shreds.

Work it out—Kickboxing or judo or running or just really hard walking. Exercise with the intention of burning off the anger.

Take action—Ask for an apology. File a complaint. Fire your doctor. Donate money to ICAN. Action moves us away from feeling like a victim.

Consider a little healthy destruction—If it is hard to access your anger, try some destruction. Pound clay or a pillow. Buy crappy china stuff at Goodwill and smash it. Get a copy of your medical records and shred them by hand or burn them.

<u>Digging Deeper</u> Take an hour and give yourself permission to rage. Do something that feels like a stretch.

<u>Partners/Family Members</u> Is the woman you love angry? Is she angry at you? Do you have the courage to face that anger? Does her anger make you uncomfortable? One of the greatest gifts we can give people is the ability to stand in the face of their anger. How about your own anger? Be honest: are there things you are angry about, that you think she did wrong? Is she being unfair to you? Is she dismissing your feelings? Give yourself space to have those feelings as well.

CHAPTER 8
YOUR BABY'S BIRTH STORY

The major role that the body's natural oxytocin plays in birth encourages the idea that birth is an experience of love...Birth is a spiritual experience simply because it is largely an act of love on the part of the body physiology and the indwelling spirit.

-Cathy Daub

In the United States, the term *birth trauma* is most often associated with lawsuits and birth injuries to babies. At least that is what comes up when you search the term. Birth injuries can be life threatening, they can be emotionally devastating, and they can produce a whole different set of trauma for a mother. Decisions that are made in the heat of labor and delivery can have permanent consequences. For many of us, the thought of a forceps delivery makes us shudder. When writing a birth plan, who ever considers that it might be necessary for a doctor to use a metal tool or vacuum extraction to force a baby from your body? It seems violent and dangerous. And it can be. It is often a decision made in order to avoid a cesarean or to deal with a baby in serious distress.

Less obvious is that on some level we know that a baby's experience of stress and emotion in those first moments must have an impact on the baby's psyche as well. Although we can't remember leaving the peace and comfort of the womb, we conceptualize birth as disruptive at best. If the event is fraught with terror and the maternal environment becomes threatening, if birth is something that is done to the baby, if the baby is separated from its mother, we fear the imprint we might leave.

David B. Chamberlain, a leading expert on birth psychology, offers this analysis of hospital birth. "The psychological problems created by this new way of American birth, although scarcely acknowledged, have been legion. Babies born in hospitals found themselves in a high-tech environment that was too cold, too noisy, too bright, and too big for them. Handling of babies was efficient but aggressive, pain was inflicted routinely; babies were separated—or isolated—from their mothers, while caregivers introduced the babies to bottles instead of breasts! Medical priorities were different from, and often in conflict with those of mothers, fathers, and babies. The majority belief among medical professionals was that babies came into the world with no sense of pain, no real emotion, and no real mind to interpret anything happening to them. This tragic miscalculation still taints the rituals of obstetrical birth in many parts of the world today."

If you believe that your baby has experienced its own birth trauma, it is important not to use this information to feed your own guilt. Think of you and your baby as a beautifully coexisting team, just as connected after birth as you were during the pregnancy. Trauma occurred throughout the system. There is no singular experience.

What hurts our babies, hurts us but what hurts us, hurts our babies as well. This can seem overwhelming until you address the other implication of this powerful connection. What heals the mother, heals the baby. Guilt serves no one. Acknowledging the hurt, and moving your healing process forward opens up enormous access to your baby's health. If we bury our hurt and pain, we ask our children to keep that secret as well.

I strongly believe that the most powerful, important thing that we as mothers can do for our children, is to take responsibility for our own healing and our own emotional well being. In fact, I believe all that we can really do for our kids is to provide them one loving, healthy, happy parent. All the wonderful options for assisting with healing your baby's birth trauma are beyond the scope of this book, but groups such as The Association for Prenatal and Perinatal Psychology and Health (www.birthpsychology.com) can be very helpful.

The emotional experience of birth trauma on a mother is also going to impact the baby and the relationship between mother and child. If you felt damaged, disempowered, emotionally wiped out by your birth, you may have felt challenged with the high intimacy demands of the first days of bonding with your baby. Those early days of establishing first attachment through touch and feeding can be layered with complex negative feelings and thoughts. Experiencing childbirth trauma can be a hit to your self-esteem. You may find yourself doubting your ability to mother instinctively if you feel that you have failed at birthing naturally. You may be flooded with feelings of guilt, shame, and humiliation. You may have bad feelings about your partner, about extended family, and about your care givers. These can have a negative impact on your first motherhood moments.

Many women who have shared their birth stories in our workshop have had babies who needed NICU (neonatal intensive care unit) care. This often means not being able to hold or nurse the baby. It can mean machines, tubes, and lots of medical interventions. For women who just gave birth, it can mean trying to manage their own care and needs at the same time as worrying about their baby's care. NICU separation can be a separate, distinct traumatic experience both for mom and for baby. Interventions that are necessary to save a baby's life may be painful, require being strapped down, or separated—not the optimum experience for early bonding.

Women begin the complex attachment relationship to the new baby very early in their pregnancy. Nearly half of all pregnancies are unplanned. Nearly a million women a year face pregnancy loss through termination. This is not an easy decision for many women and is often experienced as a significant loss. Termination may feel like the lesser of the terrifying roads ahead of them. Some women chose termination when their planned pregnancies end up with unplanned genetic defects. In fact, over 90% of women chose to terminate when genetic testing reveals that the fetus is carrying a significant genetic disease such as Downs Syndrome.

Once a woman has chosen this pregnancy and embraced this new life, she begins to create her future with the baby. She thinks about the pregnancy, the birth, and the amazing moment she gets to meet her new baby. But she also begins to walk farther into this baby's future, thinking of their life together, the child's path, and deepens the connection through the dreams a mother has for her child. All of this can be damaged by the turmoil of choices and outcomes that were unanticipated. It is hard to blame a baby for its birth, but in some ways it is also hard not to. So often after a baby is born, a mother's experience is discounted with "at least you have a healthy baby," as if only one of us can be expected to get what they need. It is a long-standing conversation, the competition between mother and prenate, on who will win the resources of a pregnancy. Wives' tales talk about the baby taking nutrients and strength from its mother. Harvard evolutionary biologist Dr. David Haig argues that this has always been the case.

"A fetus does not sit passively in its mother's womb and wait to be fed. Its placenta aggressively sprouts blood vessels that invade its mother's tissues to extract nutrients. Meanwhile, Dr. Haig argued, natural selection should favor mothers who could restrain these incursions, and manage to have several surviving offspring carrying on their genes. He envisioned pregnancy as a tug of war. Each side pulls hard, and yet a flag tied to the middle of the rope barely moves."

Mothers are held responsible for the outcome of this battle for resources as if she should always be rooting for the baby even if it comes at her expense, betting against her own survival. Public service announcements remind mothers that birth defects seem to be her fault; low birth weight and prematurity due to her choices. Alcohol and tobacco are out, but so are seafood, peanuts, coffee, soft cheese, and deli meats. Some pregnant women become obsessed with their diet, so many choices leading to possible negative outcomes. These fears of causing harm to the baby increase the anxiety and guilt a woman feels as her birth approaches.

Her desire for the best possible outcome also means she begins to plan for and prepare for a birth that honors and respects her love for the baby she is carrying. It is sad and frustrating that a woman's desire for a natural, unmedicated birth is often presented as a selfish choice, one about her desire for the experience rather than her desire for what is best for her body, the baby's health, her future birth health, her ability to nurse, and her health during the important postpartum period of bonding.

It is difficult to form close emotional relationships from a disempowered position. When we feel broken, it is difficult to see ourselves as deserving of love or capable of doing right by those we love. Women with trauma often are experiencing a great deal of guilt and shame, which takes us deep into ourselves, unable to look people in the eye. Becoming a mother is tough enough without a sense of incompetence. The emotional cost of dealing with depression or anxiety is often experienced by infants as distance or response time lags. The things we know are most important to creating secure bonding.

I hate mother guilt. When we hold on to the feeling that we have done something wrong to our kids, we are holding on to something that is destructive to our relationship with our children, not only to ourselves. If we do not forgive ourselves, we are giving our kids the message that they are being raised in a dangerous situation; that they have a less than adequate parent. It is scary being little, being totally dependent on someone else. I want my kids to know that they have the best mom. I want them to feel that their world is safe and good for the most part. I want them to see that I work hard at doing the best for them. And I want them to know that we humans are imperfect creatures. Parenting means learning to say you're sorry. It means making amends and doing it over and trying harder. Guilt is a natural feeling that lets you know that you are doing something wrong- in the present. It allows you to correct yourself. If you are speeding, slow down. Guilt over the past, things that cannot be changed, things which have been righted as best they can, is a waste of precious emotional energy. Practice letting go of guilt. It takes a lot of practice. If you were raised in a home that used a lot of traditional shame and guilt parenting, it can be a deeply ingrained habit to always be concerned about being in trouble or making mistakes.

Another impact of a rough birth on the baby is that it can make establishing nursing much harder. After a tough experience, the new mother's body is tired. Her hormones have been interfered with. She often hasn't eaten a decent meal in hours, if not days. She may be on medications whose side effects are unpredictable. She has emotional responses she is having a tough time managing. She is having trouble trusting people and herself. Even in a perfect lovely first time birth, nursing doesn't necessarily feel as natural and beautiful as you hoped or expected.

When Nate was born, we were separated for hours. He was given a bottle of sugar water and our first interaction was me trying to get him to nurse after the ease he had experienced with a false nipple. I left the hospital supplementing him with formula, certain that I was unable to produce enough milk. I have always had negative feelings about my breasts. As a teenager, I was very flat chested and had always felt less than sexy, less than womanly. Pregnancy made me feel curvier and fuller than I ever had. I had never intended to use formula. My mother, unlike many women of her generation, had nursed all of us. I remembered her nursing my siblings. It was part of my natural birth plan. I had failed at birth and now nursing felt like a second failure. Not connected, but two things I sucked at. It happened exactly the same with Joey 16 years later. I was blamed for his weight loss and for his jaundice. I was pressured to give him formula. They wanted me to stay in the hospital to ensure his safety. It wasn't until Zach's birth that I was able to see that my body was capable of producing enough milk for a big baby. It wasn't my breasts, it was my trauma. Birth with exhaustion and surgery and drugs do not lead to natural hormonal production. It takes time to recover and catch up, and with all my kids being large babies, of course it was hard to keep up with their needs. If I had been better coached and supported, if someone had simply told me that this was normal when there is trauma, then more than anything it would not have felt like two different things and I could have seen the connection between them.

Women who have traumatic births are set up to feel like less than adequate mothers. They often are overly aware of mistakes, focus heavily on their doubts, and feel it isn't safe to trust their instincts. The wounds run deep and undermine the precious bonding process. Healing birth trauma restores the relationship between a mother and her baby. It allows them to deepen their attachment relationship. Healing helps a woman to be more emotionally available and responsive to the people she cares for.

<u>Digging deeper</u> Write your baby's birth story. If you have done a lot of work on your own story, it can be liberating to go into the story from a different perspective. What happened to you is not the same as what happened to your baby. Giving voice to your baby's story acknowledges your powerful connection. Trust yourself to know and express their story for both your healing and theirs.

<u>Partners/Family Members</u> What does this bring up for you? Have you considered this baby's experience? Do you

hold part of this story? Acknowledge the parts that were wonderful and acknowledge the parts that didn't go well.

Chapter 9
The Mess of Mothering

Birth is not only about making babies. Birth is about making mothers—strong, competent, capable mothers who trust themselves and know their inner strength.
                    -Barbara Katz Rothman

We grow up with deeply embedded ideas about birth and mothering. The idea, the experience of mother is there from before we can remember. No one ever explained mothering to us. Most of us don't give it much thought...until we become mothers ourselves.

There is the world of mothering and then there is your own mother. Our mothers are our primary attachment figures. They were our first love. They taught us to trust. They gave us safety and security, met our earliest needs. They are likely the first person who ever hurt our feelings and let us down. For most women, our relationship with our mother is a complicated one. With a few words or just a look, they can cut us to the quick. Some women were birthed by one mother, raised by another. For some their first mother is also their first tragic loss. Some women have multiple mothering roles and complex mother relationships. As adults we have sought out role models or pseudo mothers. We got one when we married. At times we borrowed other people's moms. As a therapist, I am well aware that for many women, I am a stand-in for missing or unhealthy, unsupportive mothers. My job is to be a corrective experience of being mothered to, being heard, and responded to. Most of us, even if we are close to our mothers, know that no one makes us quite as crazy as they do.

The conversation around how a woman plans to birth is often the first time she bumps up against challenging her own mother's parenting. Perhaps your own mother believes she did the "only" thing she could do. Perhaps she put herself into a trusted doctor's care and made few decisions for herself. Perhaps she fought hard for an unmedicated birth with your father in the room at a time that this was uncommon. She may have had a beautiful experience or she may have had her own birth trauma. Now, even a generation later, it can be surprising how tightly women hold to their birth story. As her daughter, choosing to take a different path can feel like disapproval or criticism. It is where individuation, separation becomes evident—this is my baby, my choice.

Was your mother invited to be in the room when you birthed? If she is not in your life, for circumstances or death or simply separated by great distance, did you wish that your mother could have been there for you when you birthed? Did you trust her to be an ally? What were you most afraid could happen? Did you share your dreams and fears with her before you went into birth? What did you not talk to her about? How about your mother-in-law?

How did her birth attitudes impact you and your partner before and since the birth?

As we move away from our intense personal response to our birth, we begin to look at broader relational and societal influences on mothering. Generations of love and loss, gender roles, powerlessness, selflessness, joy, and survival impact every woman. Bethany Webster speaks beautifully about the Mother Wound (http://womboflight.com). "The mother wound is the pain of being a woman passed down through generations of women in patriarchal cultures. And it includes the dysfunctional coping mechanisms that are used to process that pain." Our cultural mother wound is evident in not feeling good enough, a constant sense that there is something wrong with you, the sense that you must remain small in order to be loved, and guilt for wanting more in life. Each of us has an internalized ideal mother archetype of motherhood. Each of us has a history of how being mothered felt. There is the mother you promised yourself you would be. Often as a very young girl, there were promises you made to yourself. "When I grow up, I will never…" There is the mother you end up being and the process of learning to do better.

Birth brings out our deepest fears of being a bad mother. We hope we don't disappoint our mothers. Feeling criticized by them can be brutal. We ultimately come up against our concerns about the conditionality of their love and acceptance. Every mother waits for their daughter to become a mother with some hope for understanding and compassion. "You just wait until you have kids!" Until you become a mother, you cannot fully understand the depths of a mother's love, nor the enormity of the task. Our decisions about whether to have children, how to have them, and how to raise them can feel like a judgement of the choices that our own mothers made. If there is trauma, abuse, neglect, or loss around your relationship with your mother, it will complicate your own mothering journey. In response to our own mothers, we have created a vision of the kind of mother we hope to be as well as a shadow self of who we swear we will never be.

Often in pregnancy, women begin to identify their mothering tribe. In online communities, at childbirth classes, at yoga, in the neighborhood, pregnant women meet, share experiences, and begin to find like-minded women. Will you be staying home or returning to work? Will you be nursing or formula feeding? Cloth diapering or disposables? Cry it out or nighttime parenting? Circ or no circ? Hospital or home? "Natural birth" or give me pain meds. Deciding what kind of mother you intend to be by aligning along these differences can be supportive, but sadly, more often they feed the "Mommy Wars," leaving women cut off, discounted, and unsupported.

What about the other mothers in your life? Are you comparing your birth to your sister's? Are there friends who just don't get it, or said the stupidest thing after your birth? Have you stepped back from your pregnant friends because you just can't talk birth right now? Are you avoiding Facebook because you don't want to hear about

Annie's easy planned c-sect or Kate's "orgasmic" pain-free delivery? Are you just too hurt and mad to check in with the wonderful group of friends you made in your childbirth class? As you work through your birth story, don't forget to take steps to reclaim the positive mother relationships in your life.

We're in this together. All mothers have inherited generations of birth trauma. It wasn't so long ago that there was a significant risk of dying in childbirth. When we look at how slowly attitudes change, this fear runs deep in people. Just mention the possibility of birthing outside of a hospital to find out how terrified most people are of "something going wrong." We are also born to women who had fewer choices in life, in birth control, in relationships than we do. They often had no voice with their doctors or even their partners. If the woman who gave birth to you is available, it can be powerful to look into your own birth story. Babies don't remember birth, but we know that in some way they are impacted by it. You might also ask your birth mother about other births she had or her understanding, expectations around birth. What were the stories that were shared about birth in your family? Were there losses? Were there struggles to get pregnant? What was said about women who didn't have kids? What are the stories of adoption or unplanned pregnancies in your family? These are strong influences in how birth was talked about around you before you even knew about birth.

I know that my mom was a strong advocate for natural childbirth and felt extremely confident in her body's ability to grow and begin new lives. My mother's first birth was my brother, whom she had out of wedlock and gave up for adoption. She married my father and got pregnant with me only 6 months after she had to say goodbye to him. Her first child was a shameful secret, an enormous sacrifice, and an unspeakable loss. I imagine her pregnancy and birth with me barely a year later brought up complicated feelings for her. I know that in huge and subtle ways, somehow, it all affects me and my births and my feelings about mothering, too.

We can trace generations of birth stories, complications, death in childbirth, infant losses. No matter what romantic notions we have about the good old days of birth, there have always been a lot of bad outcomes. Your personal family tree is impacted by the politics and economics of the culture in which birth occurred.

Did your ancestors birth in servitude, in slavery, in war, in relocation camps, in poverty? Theories of trauma informed therapy teach that trauma and abuse impact us at a DNA level, accumulative layers of stress. Women of color have been shown to have an increased risk of negative birth outcomes even with higher income and education because of the impact of the enormous stress they face from living in a racist society.

What do you know about your mother's or grandmothers' or great grandmothers' birth experiences? Where would they have birthed? Did they birth at home or in hospitals, medication free or under great sedation? Did they lose babies or suffer miscarriages? Were they forced to give up children or marry to protect themselves? Were your ancestors slaves? Refugees? Indigenous people stripped of their homes and culture? Did they live in fear, poverty, isolation?

<u>Digging Deeper</u> Write the story of your own birth. Do some interviews if you can. Make up what you don't know. Think about the time of year. Think about what was going on in your mother's life, in her environment, in her relationship. What was going on in the world? Now try writing your mother's birth story. Dig into your creative knowing. How about your partner's birth? Your mother-in-law's?

<u>Partners/Family Members</u> Write your own birth story. Interview your mother. Think about the deepest fears/concerns about birth you had before this birth.

Chapter 10
Your Partner and Your Birth

What greater thing is there for two human souls than to feel that they are joined for life—to strengthen each other in all labor, to rest on each other in all sorrow, to minister to each other in all pain, to be one with each other in silent, unspeakable memories at the moment of the last parting.

-George Elliott

The statistics say that most of you birthed with your partner holding your hand. Maybe that partner was your husband and the father of the baby. Maybe you are partners without the piece of paper. Maybe your partner is your wife who is the baby's other mother. Maybe he's that guy that knocked you up and will be your partner in parenting only. I am going to stick to partner for now. You know what I mean. Your partner is the person you had this baby with. In my experience, this is the person in the birth room least prepared for the mess that happened.

In the '70s we moved men from the waiting room to the delivery room, but over time the pressure has dramatically increased. Partners are expected to be the coach, the support person, and often when things get complicated, an advocate for their partner's wishes. In a simple birth, perhaps your partner feeds you ice chips, rubs your back, times your contractions, and cheers you on until they get to step in, catch the baby, and cut the cord. Witnessing their child's birth is an amazing experience and powerful for bonding. The problems arise when birth gets tough and goes in a direction no one is prepared for.

Birth tests our relationships. When building a strong partnership, you deepen the trust and connection by leaning on each other, being there for each other. We biologically bond to our partners, we find their presence comforting and fear losing them. Nobody makes us as crazy as the people we love. Because of this, most fights that couples have are around not feeling safe, not being certain that their partner has their back. When we feel connected and safe, we cut each other a lot of slack. Without that security, every little thing becomes a trigger. When a woman goes into birth, she is extraordinarily vulnerable. I think about us as primitive cave people. Women were most vulnerable and needed their partners and their tribe most from late into the pregnancy through the nursing years. A mother cannot fend for herself or go hunting or travel alone. She must be protected and for the sake of our human species, the tribe has continued by protecting its most vulnerable members. This vulnerability makes most women very uncomfortable. Our culture values independence and strength. It sees connection as needy.

In our primal community, women are vulnerable and need connection for safety. To some extent, fear of abandonment is biologically programmed for our survival.

In this same tribe, men were our protectors, our hunters, our warriors. They were most vulnerable when they showed any sign of weakness. His value was set by his ability to protect and defend and if he showed weakness, it put his partner and their children at risk. A weak man in the tribe might be turned out, his family taken by a stronger warrior. This leads modern men stuck with some caveman feelings that don't fit our modern reality. Their biology programs them to resist criticism, to show no weakness, to never ask for directions, apologize, or admit mistakes. OK, I don't really think that men are programmed not to ask for directions, but you can see the connection. Many men feel criticism as a threat to their attachment. They want to feel safe to be loved without risk, we want to be safe to be loved without loss. I find it helpful to consider how we can carry these cave people reactions, these impossible expectations with us into modern, complicated relationships.

Take those cave people instincts into a delivery room and watch out. This may be the most vulnerable a woman has ever felt as an adult. Her relationship with her partner may be long and secure, but they have often lived without deeply relying on each other in such an intense way. On the other hand, birth is a place where men often feel under prepared. They are asked to be emotionally responsive and available. They are asked to defend and protect in an arena where they have little power.

I admit, my partner conversation just went all male/female traditionally gendered right there. Not all men are afraid of criticism, not all women struggle with abandonment issues. In lesbian couples, gender roles are often more flexible but there is still one person giving birth, and all that entails, and one person doing the support role, and all that entails. And our gender socialization shapes us and our relationships.

Many couples bring birth trauma with them into counseling. It can be a raw spot in their relationship even years later. It is such a powerful and intense time and mistakes that get made in those hours often are hard to undo. There is your experience and there is your partner's experience and they are not the same. For first time parents, this is the experience that transforms them into parents. This is the big moment. In the months following the birth, many couples are too tired, too overwhelmed to even get a chance to compare notes. Couples don't get a chance to talk about their transformation, becoming parents, or their experience of the birth.

It can be very risky to open up about the hurts and disappointments around your birth with your partner. Often the piece of the experience that you are having a hard time letting go of has to do with not feeling heard, not feeling supported, not feeling safe. Your partner may have let you down by not believing in you or not standing up for you. They may have made decisions that go against what the two of you had decided or planned on. In the heat of things, it may have felt like the person you needed the most let you down.

Tina came into therapy with her husband unable to

let go of the fact that he had missed most of the birth, having fallen asleep in the middle of the night. His insistence that the midwife had sent him to rest, that he was sorry, that he would have been there if he'd known did nothing to appease her. She felt he had left her and was finding it hard to trust that he had her and their daughter's best interests at heart.

A woman I know, who cares deeply about birth, was deeply disappointed when her husband refused to participate in their child's birth. He had always hated the sight of blood and felt he couldn't get over his squeamishness. There was no place that they could find compromise or partnership around birth. He kept his distance both physically and emotionally through the birth and missed much of both the scary stuff and the wonderful stuff.

Another couple I worked with lost their first child. In the middle of the night, Sarah had sensed something was wrong and her husband had convinced her that she was overreacting. When they found out the next day that they had lost her, Sarah was convinced that it was her husband's fault and that had they gone to the hospital the way she wanted to, things would have worked out differently.

Many couples struggle with decisions that were made about medical interventions. If a couple has taken childbirth classes and written a birth plan, standing by those decisions once things get complicated can be difficult. During birth, many women go quiet, deep inside, and communication can be very difficult and limited. They trust their partner and their care team to give them space and time to get to where they need to be. When doctors need someone to make a decision, partners are often shocked to be called to make major decisions as the next of kin, to consent to medications or even surgery in what always feels like a life threatening emergency...even when it isn't.

Sometimes medical decisions made before the birth can feel like they are responsible for the outcome. If these decisions were not made in solid partnership, they can come back to haunt a couple. Who picked the provider? How did you decide where to deliver? How much preparation or education did you have? Did you cut corners? Were you under too much stress?

Things got said. Agreements got broken. Tempers flared. People were tired and overwhelmed and scared and totally out of their element. When women work back through the details of the day, it can be something as simple as the wrong music, forgetting the plan, a strong smell, even bad breath that can seem unforgivable. The person birthing often isn't allowed to eat anything, may be strapped down to monitors, or have her movements limited by IVs. She is naked and exposed, making crazy noises and may even poop in a room full of people. Any frustration, any yawn, any discomfort her partner expresses seems unjust. In the middle of a rough labor, the simple fact is that only you had a person fighting to come out of your body one way or another. No other experience in the room can compare.

There is your partner's story of the birth, and you might not be ready to hear that yet. Melissa shared her story with me. *Just before I went under, the lead obstetrician said, "possible fetal demise" to a physician that was entering the room to assist in response to the page moments before. The room was chaotic and terrifying—the panic was palpable. So much so that I woke up in the exact state I went under in—absolute panic and fear, wondering if my baby had lived.*

There were multiple complications that followed and I spent some time in the ICU before I finally got to the long-awaited moment where I got to see my sweet baby. As my partner handed my son to me he said, "Man, I'm so glad they changed medicines. I was really nervous about going in there. I guess it was meant to be." And it slayed me. I had just spent the last eight hours waiting to see my baby, drifting in and out of consciousness, being pumped full of IV drugs to control my heart rate, then my blood pressure, then my bleeding, wondering what he looked like, recounting the trauma that had just unfolded and wondering what in the world had just happened to me, my body, and my baby and he feels relief?

Trauma within a couple can damage their relationship. Issues of trust and intimacy can be tough to repair. In those early days, the path begins for handling parenting together. This may be just a bump in the journey or a bump on top of a long string of struggles.

Some couples struggle with their sex life after birth. It is one thing to know about the birth canal and the role a vagina plays in it, and another to watch/experience what it is capable of. For a new mother, the physical recovery can take longer than the anticipated six weeks and if she has birthed vaginally, her body is dramatically altered. She may have torn or been cut. Cesarean births are major abdominal surgery, with possible medical complications as well as emotional ones. A new mother may have body image issues or a change in her physical responsiveness. Her partner may have a hard time getting past what they saw in birth or may have a hard time getting past the changes. Add both parents lack of sleep and mom often feeling "touched out"by the intense needs of the newborn and sex for new parents is often disrupted.

Many women I know who have had birth trauma or postpartum depression have a powerful fear of getting pregnant again. This can be irrational. One woman I know used condoms while on the pill and still resisted having intercourse because she was uncomfortable with the risk. Other women I have known have wanted permanent birth control, sterilization, because they are certain that they will never want to go through birth again. While you have the right to make this decision for yourself, waiting until some healing of the trauma is done helps to ensure that it is the right decision for your future. Many older women have come forward when they learn about my Birth Stories workshop and admitted that they had hoped to have more children but their traumatic experience took that away from them.

Couples who have struggled to get pregnant or

who have had pregnancy losses can be surprised by the next set of struggles, having their eye on the prize of having a successful pregnancy. Years of infertility issues come with their own trauma, medical distrust, relationship wounds.

The first year of the first child is the hardest on partners. They often feel less connected to their wife and must create a clear role for themselves. She moves closer to the baby and away from them. If she has had a rough time emotionally, she may be unavailable to anyone. The transformation to being a mother is enormous and it can take a while for couples to reconnect after such growth.

The first year of the second child is hardest on mothers. They often feel they are letting everyone down. There is not enough to go around. The first child gets less of them with the new baby and the new baby gets less than the first one did in infancy. There is seldom baby massage for second babies. After second babies, mothers can face overwhelming guilt about not being able to be there for either child the way they want to, and partners can get neglected.

Even if your partner was right next to you throughout the birth, your stories are distinct. Your partner didn't experience what you did, and in some way will never fully understand what you went through. When the time is right, when things have settled a bit—being honest and open about everything that happened for both of you can lead to more intimacy and can be powerfully healing. There are two pieces to the story of what happened with your partner and the birth. There is the part inside of you and the part between the two of you. There is the complexity of your experience, your feelings about how your partner acted during the birth.

<u>Digging Deeper</u> First write the letter that lets your partner have it. Express it. Get it out. Say whatever you want to say. This can be really hard because it will feel mean and risky, but this version is just for you. Once you have gotten it all out, this letter can be really powerful to read aloud—to yourself or to a very trusted friend or your counselor. There is an exercise called the Empty Chair where you imagine reading it to the person or even put their picture there and read it. I think there is a value in expressing everything, but not necessarily to your partner. Once you have it all out, you will be better able to see the part that is valuable, helpful, important to share. Write that letter and share it too. Tell your partner that because you love them, and because you want your relationship to be stronger, you are taking the risk of sharing something very painful with them. Let them pick how and where it happens. Ask them to listen first, then ask questions, and then be prepared to listen to their response.

<u>Partners/Family Members</u> This one's easy—do your work first, write one letter you may never share, one that you discuss. You may be in a very different place in your healing journey. If you are ready to talk about it, work on creating the safe space in your relationship for her to tell

you her story, but be patient. Just let her know that when
the time is right, you can listen with love.

Chapter 11
Trauma at the Hands of Providers

What I fear most is power with impunity. I fear abuse of power, and the power to abuse.

-Isabel Allende

The physician must be able to tell the antecedents, know the present, and foretell the future—must mediate these things, and have two special objects in view with regard to disease, namely, to do good or to do no harm.

-Hippocrates

There are likely other people in your birth story that were part of your trauma, people you remain angry with or hurt about. While your partner and mother are long-term attachment relationships, the professionals at your birth were supposed to be trustworthy due to the nature of their profession. Nurses, doctors, midwives, and doulas are people who choose this work, who studied and who have a code of ethics they follow to ensure that they, as Hippocrates said, "first do no harm." Medical professions accidentally, callously, or intentionally can be the source of birth trauma.

There is an enormous range of trauma at the hands of professionals. It is important to work through your memories and pull apart the details of what happened from the impact it had on you. You will find raw spots in your story around something that was said to you or a procedure that went wrong or the way you were treated. This may be something rude, something unexpected, and it might be abusive, unethical, or perhaps malpractice.

Your feelings about what happened are valid even before you figure out if there is something you want to do about your feelings. You have a right to be angry or hurt about the things that were said or done to you. Don't discount those feelings. Honor the truth of your own experience. Allow yourself to feel the hurt, be angry, face how betrayed or violated you feel. There is room to consider the other side of the story when deciding how you want to move forward, but the first step is acknowledging the impact of what happened had on your birth story.

Harsh treatment can happen when things are stressful and moving fast. Perhaps someone said something rude or insensitive. Perhaps decisions were made that you don't feel you consented to. In the waves of labor it is natural to move through levels of alertness. You may have been rushed, unheard, or yelled at.

Your doula might not have come as soon as you needed her or she may have said something hurtful or judgemental that you can't get out of your head. There may have been an unsupportive nurse at your birth or the doctor might have been disrespectful. Sometimes it is just someone you didn't even know would be a part of your birth, a student or the on-call doctor or the lead nurse.

Many women interview providers and do a great deal of research before deciding how and where to deliver. Hospitals and birth centers are competing for a very lucrative business with beautiful suites, special services, and gourmet food.

Some women go with the doctor who has been doing their yearly exams without considering their doctor's philosophy about birth or whether their doctor is a part of a large group practice with rotating on-call schedules or if they deliver at a hospital with a very high first time cesarean rate. Perhaps you had a medical condition that limited your birth options. Many women, due to insurance, finances, or location, have no choice in where or with whom they have their baby.

However you came to birth where you did, however you ended up with the people who were around you, providing care at your birth—you put yourself in their care, you trusted them to do their job, and to keep you and your baby safe. For you, this was a sacred, amazing, powerful experience. For some of them it was just a work day and maybe a crappy one at that. Some providers are able to keep sacred the birth space. They do their own processing and self-care in order to be fully present to the moment you are creating, able to respond to both their professional responsibilities and your emotional needs. Some are burned out or checked out or frustrated. Some have professional or personal stressors that make it challenging to do their job respectfully.

In my home state of Minnesota we have a Patient's Bill of Rights which include courteous treatment, informed consent (in terms and language the patients can reasonably be expected to understand), the right to refuse treatment, and the right to be free from maltreatment. Most states have some form of this although sadly, the U.S. has been unable to pass a Federal version. These rights can be valuable when considering whether or not to file a grievance with the state or hospital or board.

Birth trauma has often been referred to as birth rape. I hate when the media pits women against each other and know much of the disagreement about the use of this term was generated to create tension. Who gets to define what is rape? What trauma is "bad" enough? Of course the term is powerful. For many survivors of sexual assault, this may seem exaggerated or inflammatory. The term may seem just right for a woman who has had a stranger walk into her private birth sanctuary and shove his hand into her vagina without consent.

The following are pieces of other women's stories. Read them with care.

- The nurse assumed my jar of herbs were drugs and threatened me with continuous fetal monitoring to protect my baby from me.
- The doctor insisted that my membranes had ruptured at 30 weeks and kept me in the hospital

for a month before rupturing my membranes to induce me. The whole birth was institutionalized, medicalized for reasons I will never understand.

- Without any consent or discussion, without any sense of crisis, I was given a fourth degree episiotomy, which was so hard to heal. I never got an explanation or apology for what was done to me.

- Just when I was beginning to push, the nurse yelled, "I can't hear the baby's heartbeat," and started attaching a fetal scalp electrode to my baby without explaining anything to me.

- I was aggressively held down against my wishes, the nurse wouldn't even answer my cries. She just kept screaming at me not to move while she got the monitors set up.

- Everything was panic, fear, and poor communication until I agreed to the cesarean. Then everyone was all happy and taking their sweet time. It was confusing and difficult, making me feel betrayed, like I'd been duped. I also suspect she stripped my membranes without telling me. It hurt like no other cervical check I had ever had and hours later my water broke.

- To some extent it was helpful to read them but it really opened up this wound and made me realize how frustrated I was with what happened. The notes were accurate as far as I could tell, but they didn't tell my story—at least not the whole story.

They didn't talk about how the doctor told me at her clinic before the induction how there was no added risks associated with an induction, that the contractions wouldn't feel any different with pitocin than natural contractions, nor that she actually said that an induction is easier on mom and baby. (I know now all of this is false and it is only easier for the doctor who is planning a vacation.) They didn't send the nurse notes even though I asked for them specifically. They didn't talk about how rushed everyone was to get out of the hospital (it was near the 4th of July). The doctor didn't explain anything to me before she came into the room, turned up the pit, broke my water, inserted an internal monitoring device, and said, "all done" as she rushed out of the room to start her vacation. The Op Report was the hardest to read. I just felt violated all over again when it talked about moving away my bladder and palpitating my ovaries during a surgery I didn't want, nor do I believe would have been necessary except for all the interventions.

- During a contraction the nurse started to do a digital exam. I told her to stop but she ignored me. She acted like it didn't matter what I wanted or how it felt.
- Some doctor I didn't know, who I had never met, walked in, gloved up, and put his hands in me without consent, without any discussion.

- My midwife just left me at the hospital when I had to transfer and made me feel like it was my fault that I had failed my home birth.

- The nurse just kept telling me that my body wasn't capable of birthing naturally. She said my pelvis was too small, that I had tried hard enough, but it was time to get real. She said I was putting my baby at risk and kept talking to me like I was being ridiculous.

- My midwife wasn't supportive at all. She told me, "I give that contraction a C+, you're not going to have a baby with contractions like that."

- I didn't want an epidural. My doctor didn't care. He said, "Oh you want me to cut you, yes you do. If I don't cut you, you're going to rip all over the place. Cut, cut." He then pulled the baby so hard the cord broke and did a manual extraction of my placenta without any warning or explanation. It was so horrible.

- I had a really rough labor and during the labor, the doctor suggested that I get a hysterectomy at the same time as the cesarean—I still don't quite know why. They brought the papers to sign after I had received an epidural and had been on other drugs for quite some time. I signed them. When I recovered from the birth of my beautiful son, I realized that I would never be able to have more children. I have always felt that this was gross negligence on the part of the hospital and doctor—but was never able to get any traction for a lawsuit because I "signed" the papers.

Issues with trauma at the hands of a professional may be connected to issues of abuses of power in your past. A history of abuse or rape gets wrapped up with feeling restrained or having nonconsensual contact or not having your wishes respected. If you have had someone you trusted take advantage of you, or if you have struggled with issues of assertiveness, these too can come up in birth. Many women find that they struggle to express themselves or just let things go that are bothering them or put other's needs ahead of their own.

Requesting Your Birth Records

Many women, as part of their healing journey or in preparation for another birth, will request their birth records. Your federal rights to your medical records is addressed at the Department of Health and Human Services website (http://www.hhs.gov/ocr/privacy). Basically, the best way to get them is to contact the provider and ask for their form. Then make sure you request all records, including nurse's notes—especially for hospital births. You can request records from your provider as well as the hospital/birth center. Providers can ask for you to pay a reasonable fee for copying them, supplies, labor, postage. A provider cannot deny you your records because you owe them money. You may want to request your baby's records as well since the moment they are born, their own chart is started.

It can take a while, and many people end up requesting them a few times before actually getting the records. Often a few pages will be released and you'll need to let them know that you do actually want all of your records.

Before reading your records it is important to figure out what you need, expect, or fear from them. They won't be rich in details. They will be mostly medical terms, lists of measurements and medications, and interventions. Because the medical profession uses records to justify billing and to protect themselves as well as recording the facts, you will not find much in the way of story or explanation.

Many women find requesting their records gives them a sense of closure or clarity. Many women find details they find disrespectful or insulting. You may be labeled obese or difficult. They may say you refused something or agreed to something you don't remember. There can be nasty surprises of things done or decided that you were not aware of. You may have your hugely complicated path to birth told in two lines of medical facts. The biggest day of your life being talked about like it was "just another day at the office" can be rough.

- My records made it sound like an uncomplicated "run of the mill" cesarean. In reality, I had a plethora of complications that nearly took my life.

It was painful to read through them. So much information was missing that I began to wonder if the birth I remember was even real.

- I was "out" during my cesarean so it helped me to visualize what happened.

- It was helpful to me. It made me confident in my decision to switch providers. The story the notes told was much different than my memories and the story the doctors were telling. Everything according to the notes made me a perfect VBAC patient after being told I could never birth a baby.

- My notes were incredibly helpful to me! A week long induction, plus trauma, plus whatever meds that caused my brain to have little recollection of the recovery, means I needed the notes to fill in some things. I got nurse's notes, all sorts of charting, OB notes, everything. I'm kind of obsessed, but I still read them on a fairly regular basis and have had two successful, amazing VBACs since.

- I requested everything and got everything. It was my midwife, that left a lot out, and the OB that wasn't really honest in the notes in my opinion.

- They came completely disorganized (nurse's notes from hour one, next is an OB note from hour 7, next is a nurse note from hour two, etc). I can't make heads or tails of it. As part of my healing process, I handed them over to my husband and asked him to write me up a "book report." Asking for them, and asking my husband to help me understand what happened, helped. Still not quite at the point where I'm ready to read my husband's summary...

- My records are actually fairly accurate, even down to the things I said. The only things that were not entirely the truth was that I was losing steam pushing (I could have pushed forever if they would have had the patience), and that there was no mention of the anesthesia issues (with my epidural only working partially on my left side, taking it out and trying to do a spinal for the cesarean, failing to place the spinal correctly, so going back to the epidural space, jacking the medication so that it went so high it paralyzed my vocal cords and breathing, and then wearing off so fast that I felt all of the stitching—they basically left out specifics from the OR).

- They were mostly just reports from the actual surgery and notes from the doctors and anesthesiologist. Nothing really about labor and no nurse's notes, plus I was induced, and there wasn't much of anything about that. The missing portion is where most of my questions are!

Your records are not the truth of what happened. They are a snapshot, the medical profession's story of your birth. They can be helpful, they can be painful. They may give you answers or they may only give you more questions. For many women, knowing that they exist means it is important to read them.

If you feel like there are big errors in your records, especially if you are working on getting permission to attempt a VBAC, HIPAA gives you the right to request a change be made to them if it is inaccurate or incomplete. You also have the right to have a statement of disagreement be added to your records. Not sure if that would be helpful, but it is nice to know what your rights are.

Whether you request your records or not, working through birth trauma with care providers is important for your future as a mom and as a patient. It is important to get to a place where you have resolved some of your feelings of distrust and betrayal. You will need to be able to trust care providers with your baby. You will need to go to hospitals and talk assertively to nurses. You may want to have another baby. You may end up in an emergency room for a loved one.

Personally, a final lasting impact of my birth trauma 30 years ago is that I still freak out about the anesthesia mask. I am OK with doctors, nurses, and hospitals, but not that horrible feeling of having the mask strapped on to my face. Luckily it was manageable when my toddler needed to be put under to have an almond removed from his lung. Luckily I was able to get my wisdom teeth removed while awake using lots of good drugs. So far, I haven't had to face surgery again and if I did, they would just have to use a ton of tranquilizers to get my cooperation.

Birth trauma has a tendency to make our brains rigid. In protecting ourselves, we often make broad judgements. Remember that one bad experience doesn't mean that all nurses are cruel or all doctors are rude or all hospitals are bad.

Digging Deeper After you have given a great deal of time to honoring your feelings around your birth experience, you may decide that there is something you want to do. You may want to have a conversation with your provider and let them know how you feel. You might want to write a letter to them, to their board, to the hospital. Some letters are to be mailed, others are just for you. If you feel like it was malpractice, even if you just wonder, you may want to have a conversation with an attorney. Many lawyers will give you 30 minutes for free to talk through your case. If you are feeling unresolved about a particular provider, start by writing them a fully honest letter. Spill your guts. Then let someone you trust read it and decide if there is more to do.

Partners/Family Members This is one area where your experience is most likely to be very different than your partner's. Often you were witness to things she didn't even know happened, both good and bad. Your unique experience may leave you extraordinarily angry at a provider, and perhaps not feeling like you have a right to be. You may not have had your rights violated, but it is still acceptable for you to consider writing a letter of complaint or filing a report about what you witnessed. Do some work on your own experience first, then consider options for addressing your concerns, then share them with your loved one. Don't be surprised if she is shocked, worried, or uncomfortable with your plan.

Chapter 12
Wounds to the Spirit

That is the real spiritual awakening, when something emerges from within you that is deeper than who you thought you were. So, the person is still there, but one could almost say that something more powerful shines through the person.

-Eckhart Tolle

Read this or don't. In one short chapter I am going to try to cover the complicated relationship between birth and religion/spirituality/New Age/atheism...without offending anyone. I considered just skipping it, but after addressing the other levels of impact, there is just still something missing. (Full disclosure—I am a fallen away, angry Catholic with a lot of New Age influences who currently defines herself as a spiritually sensitive atheist.)

No matter what your spiritual beliefs are, there may be a part of the impact of your birth that affects your relationship with the divine. Your spirituality is God as you know them, your beliefs about how the world works, your ideas about wrong and right and justice and forgiveness. When I speak to the spiritual costs of traumatic birth, I mean both how you make sense of your birth in relationship to your religious beliefs as well as to your deepest values. Birth is spiritual because it is our connection to the past and to the future. It touches our ideas about beauty and love. We bring our intuition, insight, guts to birth and mothering. There is nothing more powerfully creative than bringing forth a new life.

Unresolved trauma to our deepest beliefs can show up in how we feel about ourselves. It can change how we deal with the larger world around us. It can shake our sense of security. This is a time of enormous spiritual transformation. Becoming a new mother and creating a new life changes everything. Somewhere in there is the impact of the path you took to becoming a mother.

Spiritual trauma can look like anxiety or depression. You may feel more suspicious, more guarded with the world. You may feel shaken in your trust that people are basically good. You may feel like you have lost hope in the future, or faith in people. It is important to take a moment and consider the impact your birth has had on how you see the world and how you see your place in it, how safe you feel.

Our beliefs about why bad things happen are often deeply influenced by the spiritual tradition we were raised in, even if as adults we move away from those beliefs. Issues of fate and responsibility are around us all the time. Karma. God doesn't give us more than we can handle. "When Bad Things Happen to Good People." What goes around, comes around. There is a reason for everything. Laws of attraction. All of these are subtle but powerful messages.

Lindsey J. Wimmer, in her blog post "A Blog About Blogs" on her site *Stillbirth Matters,* speaks to how this happens when women lose their babies. "We are often referred to the wisdom, beauty, and perfectionism of God or Mother Nature or similar higher powers. You are telling us that God believed that your child was worthy to live, but mine wasn't. You're telling me that Mother Nature likes you more than she likes me."

Why do you think the trauma happened? How do you make sense of what happened during your birth? Do you feel like you must have done something wrong? Do you think that the people who let you down will somehow pay? Deep down, do you have feelings of guilt or vengeance? Does it have to be someone's fault? Do you think that your thinking or doubts or lack of faith may somehow have caused what happened? Do things like this always seem to happen to you? Feel like you can't catch a break? All of these reactions are deeply connected to how you think the world does, or should, operate.

The human brain looks for patterns and makes meanings and puts things together in a way that creates a story. Some stories make us feel stronger and some stories make us feel worse. We have victim stories and stories of conquest. We quickly judge if things are good or bad, right or wrong. Our society strongly teaches that things always work out for the best. This can help us live with our disappointment, or it can discount our hurts. Many of the "stories" we know are fiction. Movies and books are written with drama and lessons in mind. Storytellers create parables about how life works. We root for the good guys. We know it will end and the music will play and it will make sense.

Take some time to journal about those feelings or talk about them with someone you trust. Are your feelings in line with what you really believe? Do you honestly think that this is how things work, or does it just feel like it? Address those conflicts or inconsistencies. Where do those messages come from? What did your family and your history teach you about pain and suffering?

As a mother, this person you brought into the world is connected to your ancestors and your future descendants. They are a unique combination of two sets of genetics. You have created a person totally unique, different from any other possible combination. When you think about your place on this path, what comes up for you? Do you feel hopeful about the future? Do you worry about the world your child is inheriting? Does your giving birth feel like a gift to the planet or a crushing responsibility? What do you see in your child's spiritual future? What traditions or beliefs do you plan on passing down? What things are you determined to change for them?

For adopted parents, or those who have left their family of origin, feelings about that connection can be wrapped up with feelings of self worth, abandonment, loss. The child you gave birth to is genetically yours, but it is also your parent's grandchild. Your feelings about the relationship of your child to history is deeply connected to how you think the world does, or should, operate.

During your birth, was there ever a time when you feared that either you or the baby's life may have been in jeopardy? Whether that concern was realistic or not, those thoughts may have come to mind during your birth. What did death mean in that instance? What did you fear? How are your thoughts and feelings about the afterlife different as a mom or for your child? What decisions or deals did you make in the face of the risk of death?

My own mother remembers being very afraid that my sister wasn't going to make it during her birth. She was a "blue baby," struggling to breathe after birth, slow to respond. This was her fourth birth, not at all what she expected. She remembers that she made a promise to herself, to the baby, perhaps to God, that all she was asking for was a living child. Moving forward as a mother, she and my sister have had interesting conversations around what my sister experienced as low expectations that my mother felt was simply contentment.

What impact will your brush with death have on you, on your baby, on your future? Will you take more chances or less? Do you feel there is a reason you lived? Were you lucky or were your prayers answered? If you have lost a baby or another loved one, does that mean you're unlucky or that your prayers were ignored or that there is some other meaning to the loss? What do you do with that? How can your beliefs serve you rather than wear you down?

When you think of the spiritual aspects of birth, do you think peace and calm and perfect? Is there room in your view of spirituality for pain and suffering and swearing? Is spiritual always quiet?

In Christianity's not so distant history, the pain of childbirth was considered women's punishment for the whole garden of Eden thing—Eve and the apple. Much of the history of childbirth education has been about changing the expectation that natural birth means suffering.

If you are a person with a faith tradition, what do you believe about forgiveness and justice, about what you deserve? Is there a grand plan, is this what was meant to be? Were your prayers answered?

Are you mad at God? Disappointed? Are you furious that no one rescued you, protected you from this outcome?

It may help to go to the person that you consider your spiritual guide—your priest or rabbi, your minister or yogi—and have a tough conversation with them about your experience. So many women, who regularly attend services and who give their time, who volunteer in their religious community, never let their community be there for them. Ministers are beautifully trained professionals who get to be the voice of your religious heritage. They are more than willing to tackle some big questions. I have often recommended that a client request a meeting with their minister or their priest, and I have found these sessions enormously positive. This is different than therapy, ministers get to tell you stuff and make recommendations and share values with you in a way we therapists cannot.

If you don't recognize a higher power, if you consider yourself an atheist, your spiritual side may relate more to the beauty and love you see in the world, your sense of ethics and living with integrity. Those issues too can be challenging when faced with trauma. And if you are an atheist, there is a good chance that you were raised in a faith community. Even if you no longer agree with those beliefs or values, they can have an enormous impact on your gut reactions. You might find yourself struggling with what you intellectually believe about how the world operates and emotionally how you are feeling about how the world works. Do you wish you believed in some karma, some other worldly justice that would make you feel better? Do you miss the rituals or the community that once felt supportive? Consider both your current relationship to the divine and the impact of being raised in a family, in a community, in a culture that may see things differently. Consider how you would have handled this differently if you believed. Consider what your mother would suggest. Would she want you to pray, to have faith, to forgive? How is forgiveness different as an atheist?

Digging Deeper Write a letter. Write to God or write to Mother Earth or write to the Universe or your baby. Write about the meaning of life and of suffering.

Partners/Family Members What's your story? How does your experience of the birth impact your spirituality? Who do you need to write to?

Chapter 13
Emerge: Healing Your Community

The need to pursue healthy birth options and birth rights for women and babies doesn't end with our own births for women will always birth after us.

-Desirre Andrews

As my sufferings mounted I soon realized that there were two ways in which I could respond to my situation—either to react with bitterness or seek to transform the suffering into a creative force. I decided to follow the latter course.

-Martin Luther King Jr.

I was a very young new momma in 1984 when I suffered what I did not understand to be birth trauma. No one talked about my birth and I had a healthy baby. I don't remember having any real issues with birth in the 18 years between Nate's birth and starting to work on my trauma. I suspect that I was "fine" with birth. I went to one ICAN meeting when he was an infant and didn't talk to anyone and never came back. All I can say about that is somehow I knew I was hurt and I didn't have the right words. I had opinions and values, but I don't believe I could really bring my whole self to the idea of birth while harboring my unidentified and unresolved trauma.

I attended a good friend's birth in 1998. It was time I was conscious for a birth—except maybe my own. Vicki was single and I was her birth coach. I rubbed her back and held her hand and I got to cut the cord. I also almost passed out a couple of times. Susan, her doula, who four years later would be my doula—and the person who identified my own trauma—loves to tell the story that she had never lost a dad but that day I almost fainted. I don't think that was about trauma. I think it was mostly the fact that Vicki kept turning the heat up. But it was certainly messier, smellier, more intense, and longer than my antiseptic surgery experience had been.

If I had not asked Susan to be my doula, if I had not wanted a VBAC, if I had not chosen to have more children, I think I would have gone on being "fine" with birth. And I think that I would have been a really terrible therapist around anything birth related. I guess I would have been the "at least you have a healthy baby" kind of therapist. Having more babies and wanting to birth naturally brought me to a whole new world of therapy, community, and motherhood.

I believe that women who resolve their birth trauma hold a powerful place in the motherhood community. When we say, "how was your birth?" we are asking for honesty. We stand ready to hear the whole story. We understand the complexity of birth experiences. It isn't simple. It deserves a deep discussion. Mothers are allowed to have ambiguous feelings about what happened. When you work through your birth, when you find compassion for yourself, it offers enormous compassion to others.

Dealing with my birth trauma has made me a much more supportive friend and a much better therapist. It has allowed me to share deep parts of myself with strangers online, in my workshops, and through my writing. I think back to my earliest research into the world of birth trauma. There was nothing online. There were no books. The term was unheard of in the therapy community. I just started. Women at cocktail parties, women I had known since childhood, family members in their 70s shared their secrets when they heard what I as working on. The fork in the road was deciding if my work could help others even when I had more questions than answers. So I kept asking questions. I have never regretted opening myself to the wisdom of other women's stories.

As you move forward with your healing, you may find your passion, your anger, your sense of injustice cools. In healing, you have a right to return to the things that mattered to you before your birth or to pick new passions for your future. A strong sense of healing is knowing that your birth story is complete and that it no longer impacts your daily life. Healing means having a choice about how and when to deal with the past. Healing means that you have the right to never think about birth trauma again. At some point it just gets to be what happened, it becomes your past.

As you move forward, you may find that your passion, your anger, your sense of injustice actually grows.

As you hear other women's stories, as you do the research, you start to realize that your story isn't the only one. It is a societal trauma, a community injustice. You may start to connect birth issues to women's health care, to choice, to violence toward women, to children's health care. If your healing is calling you to pick this battle, welcome to the club.

Your experience makes you a powerful ally and advocate. I think my training in psychology has been helpful to me in understanding trauma reactions, as well as healing modalities, but I strongly believe that there is no more powerful gift any person can give than witnessing another's story.

When you feel resolved about your own story, you find it easier to be present to other's stories. You will be able to offer a mother who has had a rough birth the chance to have your full attention to her pain. Witnessing another's story means not judging, not fixing, and letting the story come. It helps to have Kleenex. Lots of Kleenex. And lots of time.

Perhaps you are interested in something more organized. Perhaps you want to fight to make sure things are different for the future. Perhaps you want to share your story with a bigger audience. Perhaps you have found a calling in the birth community.

Many women I know with a history of birth trauma have gone on to be doulas or midwives or labor and delivery nurses or childbirth educators or prenatal yoga instructors or massage therapists. Most of my colleagues in the birth trauma or postpartum depression therapy community first came to the work because of their own experience and then opened themselves to understanding the full breadth of challenges mothers face.

Here is a sampling of what some of my heroes, women with messy histories, have created.

Liz Bender Handler had an emergency surgical birth in 1979. Her journey to avoid a repeat c-sect and her commitment to support other women led her to found ICAN. The International Cesarean Awareness Network, Inc. is a nonprofit organization whose mission is to improve maternal-child health by preventing unnecessary cesareans through education, providing support for cesarean recovery, and promoting Vaginal Birth After Cesarean. Today ICAN serves women in over 100 chapters in the U.S. and many countries around the world. They support women sharing their stories through in-person meetings, private email groups, private Facebook pages, online support groups, and educational seminars. For more information go to http://www.ican-online.org/.

Solace for Mothers is an organization designed for the sole purpose of creating and providing support for women who have experienced childbirth as traumatic. Solace for Mothers provides support for mothers, as well as education and support for their family, friends, and care team. Birth trauma is real and can result from an even seemingly "normal" birth experience. (http://www.solaceformothers.org/)

White Ribbon Alliance is a global network of maternal health advocates campaigning for more resources and the right policies to prevent the deaths of women in pregnancy and childbirth, while holding governments and politicians to account for their promises of action. It was launched in 1999 based on the midwifery experience of Theresa Shaver. They work to educate citizens and governments about maternal health care situations around the world. (http://whiteribbonalliance.org)

PATTCh is a collective of birth and mental health experts dedicated to the prevention and treatment of traumatic childbirth. PATTCh began in 2008 when founders Penny Simkin, Phyllis Klaus, Annie Kennedy, Teri Shilling, Sharon Storton, and Kathy McGrath met at Penny's house in Seattle and created this powerful vision: We envision a world where women, infants, and families experience optimal physical and mental health in pregnancy, childbirth, and postpartum. (http://pattch.org)

After the birth of her son in 2011, Cristen Pascucci left a career in public affairs to study American maternity care and women's rights within it. She is an advocate for mothers, vice president of ImprovingBirth.org, and co-founder of a U.S. legal advocacy network related to childbirth. She works closely with leading national advocates, organizations, and birth lawyers to promote better treatment of women in childbirth. See more at: http://birthmonopoly.com/about.

Improving Birth is a collection of mothers who believe that they "are a cross-section of the 9 out of 10 American mothers whose bodies and babies have been put at risk by non-evidence-based maternity care." Started as a local group of moms from San Diego, they expanded to thousands upon thousands of supporters, contributors, and members around the world.
(http://www.improvingbirth.org)

Jill Arnold is a consumer advocate who founded The Unnecesarean in August 2008 as a collection of big baby birth stories, as well as women's accounts of their cesareans and VBACs. After refusing a planned cesarean for suspected macrosomia based on a 38-week ultrasound estimate of fetal weight, she gave birth vaginally to a healthy baby and later found that the Midwives Model of Care better met her needs as a pregnant woman. The final post on The Unnecesarean was on August 8, 2012. See more at: http://www.theunnecesarean.com.

CesareanRates.com, launched February 9, 2012 by Unnecessarean creator Jill Arnold, is a snapshot of online cesarean rate reporting in the United States. The site compiles the most current hospital-level data accessible to the public online, whether reported directly by a state's department of health or gathered from state hospital association websites via pull-down menus.
(http://www.cesareanrates.com)

The Shape of a Mother is a beautiful website created by artist and single mom of two, Bonnie, that is full of photos of real women, real mothers. "It is my dream, then, to create this website where women of all ages, shapes, sizes, and nationalities can share images of their bodies so it will no longer be secret. So we can finally see what women really look like sans airbrushes and plastic surgery. I think it would be nothing short of amazing if a few of our hearts are healed, or if we begin to cherish our new bodies which have done so much for the human race." (http://theshapeofamother.com)

Those are just some of the best! There are many blogs and stories and groups that have formed out of women's stories. Becoming a mother transforms a woman, birthing a lioness of strength she never knew she had. You may be shocked as your new strength is directed at birth trauma or childhood politics or education or poverty or being a great mom. What makes birth and parenting so painful is also what makes it so important. These are not casual topics. These are the core of our personhood.

Digging Deeper Write a letter to yourself before you started this journey. What do you wish you had known? What is missing in the world that only you can create? Dream. Draw. Be bold. As you release the pain, what is calling to you?

Friends/Family Members Who is speaking for you? What do you wish had been available? What is missing in the world that only you can create? As you come to a close on this journey what is next for you?

Chapter 14
A Story of Transformation

Did I offer peace today? Did I bring a smile to someone's face? Did I say words of healing? Did I let go of my anger and resentment? Did I forgive? Did I love? These are the real questions. I must trust that the little bit of love that I sow now will bear many fruits, here in this world and the life to come.

-Henri Nouwen

How do you know when your work is done? How do you know when you're healed?

My story started over 30 years ago in a different century; before the Internet. My deliberate, intentional healing work began over 13 years ago. The story I started with is very different from the story I hold today. I think I am healed. I don't even think I have any scars left. It's good. I am forever impacted by my births and the path that I chose after my births.

My healing has been a lot like my writing. I started alone, afraid to talk about it out loud. Then I got brave and shared my dream—I was going to write a book about the work I had been doing. I was on fire; I wrote lots and loved what I was doing and couldn't wait to get back to it. Then I got stuck. I put my writing down for a long time. It was there, on the shelf...just waiting for me.

Writing is like birthing. The conception is super fun. Then it gets really long and boring. Then it gets uncomfortable and heavy and you can't wait for it to end. And then you realize that the last part is the hardest…you have to get this thing out of you come hell or high water…it has to be birthed.

I didn't really want to write a book; I wanted to have written a book. Just like I didn't really want to birth a baby; I just wanted a baby. I wanted the book to be done and published and tell everyone and celebrate. I read books about writing, took workshops. I talked about writing. I just didn't want to sit hours and hours in coffee shops writing. There were parts of the work I was afraid to do. The work seemed daunting, intimidating, and maybe not that important. Who cared anyway?

And then someone would share their story. I am on both the national and local ICAN Facebook pages and every day women ask for support. Women ask how they will ever get over their birth or if what they are feeling is normal. And I write to them. I write to them when I wish I could just give them a whole book about what I know. Because I know that it matters. It matters that every day some new mother begins her healing journey.

People knew I was writing the book. You can only hide your ever-swelling belly for so long. They knew because I was foolish or wise enough to tell them. My kids knew. They asked a lot. "When is the book going to be done?" from children who I have to wrestle with to get them to write three page book reports. It helped when I told them that I was about 75% done and I had over 200 pages. Two hundred pages is a lot when you are 10. Damn it is a lot when you are old.

There are all the things you want to say and want to make sure you get right. There are the millions of versions and alternate endings and possible alleys to go down. At some point there is filling in the outline. You pick how much to bite off and you do the work. You do the parts that seem most important. And then you rewrite and clarify and go back over it and over it until it just kind of seems complete.

That's how I think the healing goes. For a while it comes into focus and is super important. Right after the birth. At the first birthday. If you decide to have another baby and are preparing for another birth. If you feel like the trauma is hurting you or your relationship or your parenting, then you do the work.

And then it fades. It slips into the past and it takes a backseat to all the other daily challenges and little traumas of life. And then something opens the wound or bumps into you. A friends has a rough birth or your sister has a perfectly easy birth or your neighbor signs up for a scheduled surgical birth and stuff comes spilling out.

There is the story you came here with and there is the story you leave with. I grant you a gentler story. One worn smooth. I wish you a story that gifts you with compassion for yourself and all mothers. I hope your work launches you into deep wisdom of forgiveness and growth.

Maybe your retelling of your birth story won't even be a story. Maybe it is a song or a painting or a dream that fades into the past.

Someday, you will hear a woman share her story and realize that you listened without thinking about your own birth. There will come a day when you tell your big kid the story of their birth and you do it without tears, without choking up. And that day you will see that you did it. You healed it. You moved it safely into your past.

And the story continues…

Chapter 15
My First Birth Story—Much Revised

This story was first written 16 years after it happened and now is rewritten after 13 years of other women's stories. It isn't *the* truth, but it is my healing birth story.

It is impossible to tell the story of my first birth without looking at the context into which I was birthing. Birth is a complex psychological journey which ties us strongly to our parents, especially our mothers. Inexplicably we all work through our inheritance of birth, often even as we resist it. So my birth story actually started before I was even conceived.

When I was 16 years old I brought home a cute boy from the neighborhood. He was a year older than I was, Catholic and adopted. My mother came face to face with her past and decided it was time to tell her three teenage daughters her darkest secret. When my mother was 20, she got pregnant by a man that was not my father. My father offered to marry her, but she decided that this was not the best path for them and gave my brother Daniel up for adoption. Seeing me dating Chris (dark and Italian rather than tall and Nordic) made her realize that it was possible we could bump into Daniel who had been adopted by a local family through Catholic Charities. This changed everything I knew about her and forever changed my relationship to her.

At 16 my response was very selfish. I was not her first. I was her replacement child. She married my father six months after Daniel was born and as my father always teased, I was born nine months and two seconds after the wedding. My mother had three daughters before she got her beloved (second) son. I remember praying that baby #3 would be a boy, I had assumed it natural that a mother with two daughters would want a son, but now that story had a desperate flavor.

Becoming a mother forced me to look at her sacrifice and her loss. Had she been looking for his face at every playground, every school event, at the beach for 17 years? How did she mark his birth each year? Of course when I took my first steps she thought of him. Each of my milestones must have been bittersweet.

My mother tells me that at my birth, only she and my father knew that it was not her first birth. She denied her birth experience to her doctor. And he of course pretended to believe her. When she was pregnant with Daniel, she had been sent to stay (mostly hidden) with a good Catholic family until she gave the baby up. Her pregnancy with me was the first one she got to celebrate publicly, hearing advice and encouragement, unable to share her first birth story. All of my life I had a ghost hovering over me, my mother's unspoken loss.

At 20 I found myself in my mother's shoes, pregnant and unmarried but with modern, liberated options. I got to choose. I originally scheduled an abortion, believing that was the only choice. My parents were going through a horrible divorce and I feared stressing them out, adding to their problems. My parent's divorce had been making me so physically ill that I had thrown up my birth control pills for months and was being treated for an ulcer. I kept getting sick and better, sick and better. At one point my doctor began to scope me, concerned that I had cancer. By that time my tumor had turned into a pregnancy—nearly 12 weeks before I could admit that to myself or my doctor.

I initially chose to handle this alone. That's my MO. I have to share that it was Planned Parenthood, the same agency that so many people despise, that counseled me to not make the decision to end my pregnancy alone. They made me think about it and made me promise to talk to someone before proceeding. Here's the funny thing about memories, some are so vivid and some from the same day are gone forever. I knew in the instant that if I told my mother that I was pregnant, I was choosing to have this baby and that I could never give him up. I knew the path that I was choosing. If I had wanted an abortion, then the first person I could have or should have told was my baby's father. Telling my mother closed a door. I don't know if I closed that door and then told her, or if I told her and knew that that door had closed. Mother/daughter relationships are complex and this was oh so long ago. I was so much younger, we have so much adult history since then.

I spilled my guts to my mother. When I began the pregnancy, I was failing out of college, breaking up with my boyfriend, horribly underweight, and losing my hair. I don't think I could have ever predicted the struggle I was choosing by following an altered version of my mother's life. The only options available to my mother were marrying my father and living the lie that her son was their son, or giving him up and living the lie that she had five children, denying his existence every day of her life. I had choices she didn't have. I got to continue this pregnancy alone, in public with very little shame, and continue my education as well. My mother finally completed her college degree when she was 60, a fact we are all enormously proud of. The minute I chose to continue the pregnancy, I also chose to get my shit together—excel at school, get my physical health together, and put my baby first.

I threw myself into this pregnancy. I ate, I exercised, I read, and I went back to school with a vengeance. Because I was underweight and because it was the '80s and because we didn't have fancy ultrasounds, I put on 60 pounds to make sure he was healthy. When women tell their birth trauma stories, they look back for evidence of what they did wrong and of what they did right. Because Nate also ended up with serious health issues later in his childhood, I also question whether those were also my "fault." I had x-rays because I thought I had cancer. I drank some and was in terrible health for the first trimester of my pregnancy. I wished away this baby for weeks before I chose him. Today I know that those things have nothing to do with his birth or outcome. They are just what happened. I carried a ton of guilt and fear during my pregnancy, and all I wanted was "a healthy baby."

We talked to my mom's friend Chris, a nurse who had taught Lamaze classes in the '70s. She sent us to a midwife, all of us from day one talking natural childbirth. Looking back, Chris knew little about what was changing in the world of birth, and this midwife practiced with a group of OBs who specialized in high risk pregnancies at a hospital with an ever-increasing intervention and cesarean rate. My mother had birthed all six of her children without pain medication. Only once had there been any complications, my sister had been a "blue baby," the cord wrapped around her neck in a way that scared my mother. That may be her only experience of birth trauma. In fact my sister and she have their own story to tell about how that birth experience, which I now understand to not even be particularly rare, set their relationship up for low expectations and misunderstanding. So many women felt unsupported in their choice to birth naturally because their mothers had chosen differently and felt criticized and threatened by their daughter's beliefs. My mother birthed naturally and breastfed and believed in my innate ability to do both well.

Nate was an unwanted pregnancy and then a chosen child. He was a replacement for my mother's lack of options in the same way that I had been. He was my chance to do it different. I went into birth empowered and supported and prepared for a vaginal birth. Like most women, I had never prepared for a surgical birth. That would have been bad faith, that could have jinxed things. I chose natural birth and then stepped into the world of OBs and hospitals and people who knew a great deal more about surgical birth and interventions then they did about natural births. The midwife I had was great but she was the only midwife in a large OB practice that specialized in high risk pregnancies. I got her until things got "messy," and they got messy fast.

In 1984 we didn't use as many ultrasounds as they do today. My due date was considered vague. At this point I was pretty sure of when I had gotten pregnant, but the difference of a week or two meant the difference between this baby being the "nice guy's" and the "love of my life's." Nice Guy might have hung around, Love of My Life didn't. But that is a different story and that is Nate's story, not mine to tell. I knew, or at least wanted to believe, that I was very sure about his conception. I wanted to believe that I remembered his conception, that it had been special, that he had been conceived in love. Anything less was gross and wrong. I had enough strikes against me as a mother. I needed to believe I had done one thing right. I calculated over and over again with that little wheel in the doctor's office. I knew he was due on September first. (The last piece of this puzzle wouldn't be fully solved until Nate was nearly two years old and the blood test revealed what I was (almost) certain was true: that his father was (at that point) The Love of My Life.)

On my due date, as many women do, I figured my birth would occur. I tell people that on that day I went to the State Fair, walked for six hours, had half of a beer, and waited for the baby to come. He came more than two weeks later. I went into labor naturally about 11 pm. I wasn't sure but I thought my water had broken, not the gush like it happened on every TV show, but maybe just a trickle. Nice, easy contractions building through the night. I savored not telling anyone, sleeping between them, trusting my breath and my meditation skills. I believed that I knew how to birth naturally, just as my mother had.

My mom and I went to the hospital around 7 am. Contractions steady and four minutes apart. The nurse that checked me in scolded me for not coming in earlier if I thought my water had broken. (I knew better than to go in until it was really time.) She predicted a big baby, maybe even eight pounds. OK, honestly I remember some, but not most of the next 12 hours. Failure to progress, pitocin drip, internal monitoring, dilated to two centimeters...nothing and everything happening. I wanted to be alone with my mother. I had friends and family showing up wanting to be a part of my birth, but my natural extroverted self collapsed in on itself. I surfed through contraction after contraction, resting, meditating, breathing but getting so tired. I was both internally and externally monitored. There was something strapped across my belly tight and uncomfortable and there were wires between my legs, wires going inside of me, wires that were poking into an unborn baby's head. And all of these wires connected to machines and the machines had bells and whistles and paper coming out of them and the machine said I wasn't doing it right.

So here's the weird thing about trauma. There are things that I know happened, but that I don't exactly remember. I know that I hate pitocin. I would never allow it to be used in my body ever again. I don't know why. I just know that the word makes my pulse race and I get nauseous even after 30 years. It is a good thing I am not a doula or midwife; I know pitocin isn't "evil"—it is a very powerful and useful drug—but for me it is forever wrapped in trauma. I know that whatever was happening to me wasn't "natural," and more importantly wasn't working. It is one thing to go through hell to get somewhere, it is another thing to simply go through hell to find yourself in your same location. I got tired and so did the baby. At least that's what the monitor said.

At my absolute emotional worst, exhausted, discouraged, and defeated the conversation turned to cesarean. Something neither my mother nor I had ever considered. I knew nothing. I had no idea how to decide. My mother begged them to let me have some sleep, let me take a break. Enter my first experience with "the dead baby" conversation. Risks and concerns and possibilities and fetal heart decelerations and risk of infection. I signed a consent I suppose. I must have. I caved. I agreed.

I remember being taken into the operating room alone. I have one memory carved in stone that runs in an endless loop when I talk about Nate's birth. I was counting

164

down, doped up, strapped to a table, alone when the anesthesiologist put the mask over my face and the last words I heard were, "Call Children's Hospital. There's something wrong with the baby!" and I was out. OK, I know enough about memory and trauma to know that this is a suspect memory. Who knows what happened and who cares? I have this tape running through my head and it is the only thing I have of that day. If it happened or not, it impacts my experience of birth.

MAJOR DISCONNECT. That is what general anesthesia gives you. All the memories and emotions shut down like a power outage, as if the movie ended, the curtain closed. When the curtain opens again, it is a new movie. I wake violently from anesthesia. I don't remember the first time. I remember the second time. The exact same thing happened when I was 14 and got my tonsils out. The nurse is shaking me. "Honey, wake up. It's a boy." I have no idea what she is talking about and I want to hit the snooze button. And a boy? That is also not what I expected. (Remember this is 1984 when people found out the sex of the baby when it came out of you.)

I met Nate hours after his birth. Everyone else had seen him. He had been given a bottle of sugar water, he wasn't interested in nursing, and I knew I had missed something. Something very important. I feel terrible that I have a crystal clear sweet memory of labor and a crystal clear terrified memory of going under and a pretty murky, drug-addled memory of meeting Nate.

It isn't a bad story. It isn't a happy, beautiful birth story. I can't find anyone to be mad at. My midwife handed me to an OB who was a stranger. The first nurse handed me down the line of nursing shifts. The only constant was my mom and she had no idea what I was going through. Sixteen years later when my friend Susan asked me the earth shattering question: "Have you done anything about your birth trauma?" lots of things fell into place. I realized that in 16 years my mother and I had never spoken of my birth. I called her the next day and she cried as she explained that she knew she had failed me. That she had always felt bad that she had let me down. Funny, I thought I had let her down. That part of the trauma cleared up in one conversation, one conversation delayed 16 years.

Another piece of my personal puzzle was how well I had protected myself from even thinking about the birth. I hadn't ever called the doctor or even returned for a six week visit. I hadn't taken Nate into the doctor until he was almost two months old. I just went home. I was "fine" and the baby was "fine." I struggled a great deal with nursing. Did I mention that my two week overdue baby weighed in at 10 pounds and 6 ounces? He was hungry and used to a bottle and I ended up using nipple shields which caused me to crack and bleed. Couldn't birth right and couldn't nurse right, a 21-year-old unwed mother; not the best start for any family.

Because Nate was born on the 16th of September rather than the 1st as I had expected, I was scheduled to return to school days after his birth. I assumed that given

166

the new baby and the surgery that I would have to take a semester off. My mother freaked out. She was terrified that if I stayed home for three months with Nate, I might never go back to school. She feared my becoming a welfare mom. She feared I would fall into the stay-at-home motherhood trap she was working so hard to pull out of. I just wanted some time. I was terrified. I didn't know how I was going to do it. I believed that a semester off wouldn't stop me. It worked out fine that I went back to school. I was taking mostly night school classes which were long and only met once a week so I had a pretty light class schedule. I was majoring in psychology and minoring in women's studies and my mom went to all my classes the first week, paving my way by letting anyone who would listen know that I had given birth and would be back in school in a week.

I see this as my mother's version of "back in the day women gave birth in the fields and went right back to work." That is a terrible lie told to women. Of course there were women who had to go back to work in the field immediately following birthing; SLAVES. Birth is a huge strain, costs tons emotionally and physically, and recovery following an easy birth should involve weeks of rest. Surgical birth, birth where there has been trauma, requires even longer to heal. My mother believed that I was "fine" and that it was imperative that I get back to "normal" as quickly as possible.

One caveat, my mother had not returned to college at this point in her life and she has admitted since then that she didn't see college as work. She also did promise to make life as easy for me as possible—watching Nate while I was at school and covering my rent. I don't remember how I felt. I don't remember bleeding. I know I was walking a mile to school by the time he was a month old, which seems insane today, but I was only 21 years old. Maybe in some ways, I was OK.

I remember my scar. Well I obviously still have my scar. The one they cut open once again 18 years later. I remember they took the staples out before I left the hospital. That is one reason I figured we were done. It never occurred to me that I needed to come back. Staples out, sent home, you're fine. My scar hurt, my stomach was stretched out and so ugly. No one told me that you look pregnant for weeks after you give birth. I was confused about how I felt about my body. I had created a life, and honestly as a single mom it really felt like I had created him totally on my own. I didn't like my stomach but I did have breasts, which having been almost totally flat chested my whole life did make me feel womanly for the first time. And I loved nursing. I fought hard to establish and repair our nursing relationship. I struggled with milk supply issues from the minute he was born and supplemented with formula. Given that in 1984 less than half of all moms nursed, I felt great. There was much less pressure/support for nursing and if it hadn't been for my mom, I never would have made it the nine months that I did.

I had a beautiful, huge baby that everyone adored. Nate brought my family together. In the middle of an ugly divorce, his birth was the greatest gift my family could receive. I moved on, focused on my baby. We were both healthy, we were both fine. No one ever asked me how I felt about my birth, and I locked the door to that story and moved on.

Chapter 16
The Middle Story—Our Loss

When Paul and I married in 2000, it was clear that we hoped to have children together. He had never had kids and I had struggled for so long as a single mom, we both dreamed of creating a new family. There were some worries. I was 37, he was 40. It seemed like every time you turned around there was another story that made it seem like I was guaranteed to have fertility issues. My two younger sisters both suffered infertility and in some ways I felt I had been lucky. Maybe I had gotten all I was due. For most of my life I had tried really hard not to get pregnant, perhaps I had missed the boat.

We got married in November and I was pregnant by January. We had sold Paul's house, moved to a new home, and I was repairing my house to get it on the market. I was working full time and putting in long hours at the other house. I was using lots of paint stripper. Oh, and we flew to London on a great vacation. I can give you a list of things that I think might have killed my baby. I know that's not how it works, but that's how it feels like it works. Flying, chemicals, stress, my age, Paul's age. The Universe hates me, I did something bad, it's the plan, I am being punished.

At 10 weeks I started spotting. The doctor was nice and all, but it was clear that spotting at 10 weeks almost always means one thing and there is nothing that can be done. Spotting happens after it is already done. The ultrasound simply verified what we knew. The baby just hadn't developed. The baby was silent, without a heartbeat. I counted 10 weeks but it was clear that the baby had only made it to about six. That's the part I got really angry about. Of course it was sad that the baby hadn't made it. I had walked myself all the way to this little girl's graduation party and college plans. But the part that I got really stuck on was that I had been talking to her and planning her and taking such good care of her and I hadn't known. For a whole month. I felt cheated, again. It just would have been so much easier if I hadn't walked a whole month into the future that I didn't get.

Both Paul and I were raised Catholic but find little comfort there. We are former Catholics, fallen away Christians. We both resent what the church has done to people. We both agree that dogma is dangerous. More New Agey types, hungry, and always searching for spiritual answers. Paul told me that he believed that the baby's spirit came through needing simply to be loved. It was a soul whose life journey was to experience unconditional love and that in those short six weeks, its journey completed. We had loved that baby more than it had ever believed possible and back it went, on to greater adventures, healed and powerful. Man do I love that guy! Works for me.

Passing the tissue was horrible. Nobody told me that. It was Easter morning and I had chosen to let things happen naturally. The doctor said that if nothing happened

I could come back in a week for a D&C but there was no need. "Let nature take its course." The thing no one said was that it would feel like passing glass through my vagina. This "nature" thing just keeps blindsiding me. No one said my hormones would go nuts. No one said take it easy, go slow, take some time off. It was just sad. I got that. But it was scary and lonely and it stayed with me. And once again, I just kept moving. I never took a day off of work. I didn't think healing was important.

I feared it would be my first of many miscarriages. I feared it was my new badge, that I had problems carrying a baby to term or I had infertility issues, that I would never have another child. It was a tiny trauma because I conceived Joey less than a month later. There could not have been both babies, they took up the same space. I didn't hold on to the due date because it got wiped out by the new pregnancy. The new pregnancy that had me checking for blood every time I went to the bathroom for four months...maybe five.

I don't think about that loss very often. Once, a few years ago I was meeting with a spiritual counselor... you know a psychic. Out of the blue she said, "there's another baby isn't there?" I had said three boys but of course that wasn't the whole story. "Don't worry, that baby was Joey. He just came back." And I began to sob. Once again someone had opened the pain that I was denying. I didn't think I hurt about my miscarriage. I believed that I was "fine." And honestly I don't even know if I believe in psychics. Of course I want to believe or I wouldn't be sitting in her office paying for her time. I hunger for something deeper. Something opened up and released when she told me what I wanted to believe, that the baby simply passed through and came back to me.

Chapter 17
Joey's Birth—A Healing Surgical Birth

There was not one appointment, not one decision that was made in my pregnancy that did not begin with "at your age." My chart was labeled "AMA." In my world, AMA meant against medical advice, it was how some people checked themselves out of the psych ward; against medical advice, at their own hand. I was "AMA," of Advanced Maternal Age. The whole time, from conception through birth, I was reminded that this was not what they recommended. But the first trimester passed into the second and I had my fateful conversation about birth trauma. I knew that what I was looking for was called a VBAC. Years before I had gone to one ICAN (International Cesarean Awareness Network) meeting. I know I heard some other women share their stories, but I never spoke.

A dear friend of mine had asked me to be at her birth four years before. She birthed naturally with the help of our friend Susan. Susan was her doula, I was the stand in for the daddy, a not so reliable guy who she didn't feel could support her. My friend has a horrible physical and sexual abuse history and we worked hard together preparing for the big day. I was there when Charlie was born. I got to put my hands on him as he came through the birth canal and I got to put him to his mother's breast. I got to see him be born. I got what I had been denied at Nate's birth, but because I was still in so much denial about what I had lost, what I had suffered, I didn't understand why Charlie's birth was so difficult for me. Susan teased me that she was afraid I was going to be the first "dad" to actually faint on her. But this was before any of us had talked about birth trauma.

I trusted Susan to get me the VBAC that I wanted. I wanted her at my birth and Paul agreed. He adored her the minute that they met. We put ourselves into her hands and followed her lead. I know Susan has learned a lot about birth since we planned Joey's birth, and I know that we both would chose things differently today, but we did the best we could with what we knew. Today I would tell a woman in my position to birth at home, but I wouldn't have trusted that then. If it were me today, the challenge would be picking my birth provider because I know and adore about nine of them here in the Twin Cities who I believe could have supported me in birthing Joey naturally and at home. But even home births with amazing midwives and tons of support sometimes stall.

Side note: we went to meet with a genetic counselor to discuss having amnio done on a beautiful fall day—September 11, 2001. The nurses were gathered around a small TV watching the second tower fall as we left the doctor's office, clear that our baby was fine.

Surreal. But who doesn't have a 9/11 moment etched in their mind?

Two thousand two was before everyone was obsessed with uterine rupture. That happened sometime between the boys. No one worried about it in 2002. Funny but in 2002, I had five to six hospitals to choose from for a VBAC, by 2004 there were really only two or three, today I suspect that no hospital would give me a chance at my Advanced Maternal Age with 2 c-sects for failure to progress, late term 10+ pound babies—bad odds. We prepared together; Paul, Susan, and I. Susan shared meditation tapes with me and talked me through her understanding of what might have gone wrong the first time. We went to childbirth classes at the hospital and the classes offered through the Childbirth Collective on preparing for natural birth. We trusted my body and my care providers and we let things go the way they go. I made Paul and Susan and the midwife promise not to offer me a surgical birth. No one was to say those words. I was so afraid that someone would offer me an easy way out and in a moment of weakness I would take it. That was how I saw my first birth. How unfair that no one that day could stand up to the doctor and refuse surgery or suggest alternatives. I had little choice with Nate. I wanted to be in control with this baby. I knew that a surgical birth was an option. That was my call and I planned on holding strong. No matter what.

Joey also went two weeks over his due date and they started to talk about induction if labor didn't start by

Monday. Susan suggested that I didn't have to call the midwife on Monday. She was walking a very fine line with me. As a doula she was not supposed to offer medical advice. But the only strong voice I was getting was the one pressuring me that I had to make sure my baby was OK. I couldn't just let this pregnancy go without some kind of intervention. The tide had turned, they didn't doubt my calculations. They knew he really was late and they started the scare tactics whether they knew it or not. Even as a 37-year-old professional, I doubted my ability to tell the doctors no. I couldn't imagine not doing what they wanted me to do.

Luckily labor started late Saturday night. We called Susan on Sunday and she came and sat with us and helped me labor until we were sure I was ready. I threw up in the car on the way to the hospital and we were certain I was in transition. I was having strong, consistent contractions. I felt in control and positive and beautifully supported and loved. The nurses at the hospital were great. We got me admitted and then they checked me. Two centimeters. Nothing. I had labored for almost 24 hours. I sucked. I was horrible at birth. I was broken and stupid and even with all the best care in the world, I just couldn't birth. I felt so horrible about myself. Defeated already.

They sent me home. The nurse gave me something. I don't even know what it was because she whispered in my ear, "Honey, I wouldn't take this, I'd go home and have a glass of wine and lay down for awhile." Even then, no one seemed to doubt that I could do this.

Home we went—Paul to bed and Susan and I on matching couches. Sleeping most of the night, labor mostly slowed, I decided in the morning that we should talk about surgery. I just didn't know how to have a baby naturally. Time to admit it. We showed up at the hospital at 9 am somewhat reluctantly, but at least feeling I was in control. When they checked me I was now seven centimeters dilated. Something was happening and they thought I should give it a go.

Again, I don't really remember. Maybe Paul can write this part. I have pictures of this time. Pictures of me wrapped in big white hospital blankets looking withdrawn into myself. Contraction after contraction, washing over me, naturally, supported, in control, and then I just stalled at nine centimeters. Forty hours of labor and one check said nine centimeters, the next no longer nine...who ever heard of going backwards? That was it for me. I had been laboring for most of the past 40 hours. I gave up. I remember saying, "Get this baby out of me the fastest way you know how." They got me in line for the operating room. One hernia ahead of me, I was headed to surgery.

This time I had a plan. This time I knew what surgical birth meant, I knew what I wanted, and I had faced this place both in my head and in my heart. It was not the enemy. It was not losing, it was second place. It was not the gold medal but it was the silver. I was awake and in control and supported and at peace. Susan said goodbye for a while, they would allow me only one support person in the room so Paul stayed and she stepped out. Funny, it was a teaching hospital and I think the doctor got to bring a whole slew of strangers...but I only got one. The minute that I had decided to go for the cesarean, my labor had stopped. My body knew. I simply flipped a switch and gave into Plan B. Cesareans are not the enemy. They are not by design bad or traumatic. Joey's birth was triumphant and healing and joyful. I was by this time an old momma, but this was the day that Paul became a father. I watched the whole birth through his eyes.

I hear women talk about quiet, peaceful water births or home births and I get that, but I kind of like the party that happens in the operating room of a teaching hospital. I swear there were eight people in there and I had never met any of them. They were caring and wonderful. I was given space to have this be what I wanted it to be. I don't know the doctor's name, but I will never forget him giving Joey his apgar scores: 9 and 10, the 10 that they say is reserved for doctor's children. He kept saying, "Did you see that baby? Wasn't he beautiful?" And he was. He was two weeks late and one ounce shy of his big brother's record: 10 pounds and 5 ounces. And I saw him and touched him and when we were separated for my stay in the recovery room, his daddy never left his side. And when I write this, even 13 years later I glow. That is a good birth story. That is redemption and healing.

Daddy followed him for the first two hours while I recovered. I had been awake, I hadn't been scared. I knew where my baby was. And this baby had the amazing advantage of having a daddy, something I wanted for him even more than I wanted a vaginal birth. Daddy bonded. That wasn't a lose for me, that was a win. I knew we could catch up later. No sugar water, no bottles for this one. He latched when they brought him to our room and nursed like a champ.

My first son and my second son are 18 years apart in age and have different fathers, and one was an accident and one was planned. For my first I was too young and too naive to be a mother and my second I was too old and jaded to birth easily. And their births were the same. For them, their births were the same.

I did struggle with supply. I remember how hard it was to nurse and bed share with my legs in those horrible compression things. I was still mostly paralyzed from the waist down. They tried to keep us in the hospital a day longer and "made" me start formula and scared me and made me promise to take him to our pediatrician the next day just in case. So I guess that old mommas don't get any more respect than young mommas do.

Chapter 18
Zach's Birth—The Big Win

Having a third child felt like a bonus round. I had dreamed of getting a second chance at mothering but never really dreamed I would have three kids. We weren't sure how quickly we would get pregnant again or if we were in for more miscarriages. My second sister was facing her infertility issues and again I feared it wouldn't be easy. Our goal was to begin trying when Joey was 15 months old and we got successfully pregnant the first time we tried. Of course I still checked for blood at every bathroom break, but after the first trimester we were set.

I let Susan know we were ready to try natural birth again and got her recommendations. Rebecca was the one hospital midwife who would even consider me. Actually Susan said, "There is only one person who is going to be willing to take you on and I'm not sure you're going to like her. She's pretty tough." Home birth never came up. I knew few people at that point who had birthed at home. I suppose at the time, I did believe that my VBAC attempt was dangerous on some level. The was a great deal of media at the time regarding findings about uterine rupture and VBAC risks. I was going to be 40 when this baby came and had two previous surgical births due to failure to progress, two babies at 42 weeks and over 10 pounds. I felt like I showed up in her office begging for a chance to have what I had no right to: a chance at a natural birth.

When Susan sent me to Rebecca, I knew about her bedside manner but I wasn't interviewing her, she was interviewing me. She was a tiny, 60-year-old woman with a no nonsense style. Rebecca had me request Nate's birth records which were deep in some hospital cavern. My first surgery was done with a less than optimal incision. She went through a checklist of my risks and as I watched her check through them, I could see that I was an unlikely candidate. As well as the common concerns that I had been prepared to address, Rebecca added two others. She believed that women should not gain more than 25 pounds per pregnancy. (I had put on nearly 50 with each of the other two, but couldn't exactly defend that when the outcomes had been surgery.) After agreeing to take me on as a patient, she also dropped the bomb that I just might be too educated to have a natural birth. She believed that women who lived in their heads did poorly in their bodies. What the hell was I going to do with that? Did that mean that any preparation for birth was just making it less likely?

I hated when she said that. It was in no way helpful. Here is what I wish she would have told me. Stop reading. Stop thinking about birth and researching. Don't talk to other people. Be physical. Dance or do yoga or have body work done or even lots and lots of sex. Go within. Pray or breathe or scream, but don't read. That might have been helpful. She could have told me that there were other

182

ways of learning. I might have explored Hypnobirthing or Birthing from Within and some other spiritual, heart centered birth preparation.

I left that day feeling grateful that I had a chance and would have agreed to anything. I promised to limit my weight gain and exercise religiously. And I promised to not be too intellectual, at least not for the next six months, somehow. I had a plan.

Rebecca believed that the good news was that we had two science experiments that went exactly the same way. Nearly 20 years apart and with different fathers, I had gotten the same birth. If I did the same thing this time, it was likely that I would get the same outcome. That made sense in my so logical, too educated brain. Everything that I had read (see, there I went reading again) said that it was imperative to let the baby choose their birth date. I didn't believe in due dates, but due months, and I would never interfere with this. I believed that babies ripened and dropped just as they were meant to. Except mine. I had a stubborn cervix or stubborn children or maybe I was thinking too much to allow my babies to birth naturally. (There was one serious flaw in this reasoning. Perhaps Joey had been born to a woman with a Master's degree who tackled everything as a research project, but Nate had been born to a kid who was barely passing college. My births were not my fault.)

I was supposed to convince this baby to get here early knowing full well that artificial means of induction were considered very dangerous given my history and perceived risk of rupture. Early, but not too early, induced but not medically. And thin and earth mother and relaxed, oh yeah- relaxed.

She insisted that if we were going to put this baby through a VBAC attempt, we needed to get a peek and make sure he was OK. After Joey's birth, my one request of my birth team was that NO ONE MENTION MY AGE. I was well aware that weeks after I conceived I made the horrible step into the world of 40. I knew this, they knew this. I just didn't want to be reminded every day. However, since I was of a certain age and this baby was perhaps going to be asked to do a 40-hour marathon, we did do an amnio. She trusted the doctor who supervised her. Not exactly trusted him. He could use the needle safely. If I "failed" my VBAC attempt, he could be trusted with the section. He didn't interfere with the brilliant midwives whose names were famous in town for getting women natural births against all odds. He was their beard. He covered for them. He put his license on the wall and stayed out of the way. Again, I would have done anything Rebecca asked me to do, so I got the amnio done when all I had ever heard was that they were unnecessary, risky, and that you had to be ready to take a hard look at your beliefs about abortion because once those results came in, decisions had to be made and quickly.

We talked and searched our recovering Catholic souls and decided that if only so that we could be prepared for the birth, we needed to know that this baby was healthy. And of course he was. I was 40, but that didn't mean my genes were damaged or tired. There was another unseen benefit. I wanted a natural birth. More than anything I wanted that. And as hard as I was working for that, I also had to admit that I wanted a daughter. As so many women do, I saw mothering as playing dolls, tea parties, baking, reading *Little House on the Prairie* with my daughter. I wanted to revisit the wonders of my (little girl) childhood. I loved my boys. I was a great mother. I had learned to love Legos and trucks and balls and mud and wrestling and my boys put up with some of my feminine interests as well. I wasn't going to be ruined by it, but separating my desire for a beautiful birth from my desire for a daughter was a good thing. I got the great news that the baby was perfect and healthy and male and that we should certainly move forward with my plans to birth naturally. And I settled into the sadness that was accepting that no matter what happened, I wasn't having a daughter. This was it. It was time to let go of that desire. It wasn't so bad. I had nearly six months to prepare for baby boy #3—Zach...Z for the end of the line.

The path was fairly uneventful. We didn't do classes, no more books to read. I exercised and ate right and went to work everyday. My clients guessed right away—I threw up during a therapy session and didn't want anyone thinking I was contagious. I also got so big, so fast as is often true with your third. I was savoring my pregnancy knowing it was my last. The new midwife meant a different hospital and appointments clear across town, but it was a small price to pay. When I hit the

36-week mark Rebecca told me it was time to start thinking about induction.

Thirty six weeks is considered to be (mostly) full term. Low risk. Developed. I had big babies, we knew exactly how far along I was. He needed to get here before he hit 10 pounds for me to get my best shot at the birth that I wanted. The birth I knew we both needed. But 36 weeks? It felt so wrong. It was "unnatural" to mess with this clock.

This whole risk of rupture stuff is crazy—you can't do any of the synthetic hormonal stuff. Natural induction included nipple stimulation with my breast pump which I hated, chiropractic adjustments, lots of sex, evening primrose oil, and acupuncture. I don't know what was working or not working given that I was doing everything that anyone recommended. Relaxed had gone out the window. I certainly didn't feel like I was handling this intellectually, I'm not even sure I was handling this rationally. The acupuncturist recommended trying castor oil, which rumor had it was a risky old wives tale. I think I knew that Rebecca and Susan would tell me not to, so I just didn't ask. At 37 weeks, I came home from my second session of acupuncture and poured a shot of castor oil into an orange juice smoothie and gulped it down. The theory of labor induction with castor oil is that it acts as a stimulant to the bowels, which irritates the uterus and causes contractions. The side effects from castor oil can include diarrhea and vomiting. Of course the biggest risk is that it won't work on the baby and you will end up drained, exhausted, and starving going into birth.

It worked or something worked or everything worked. At 37 weeks, my labor began perfectly and mostly "naturally." Like the other two, my contractions started in the evening but this time rather than sleeping off and on for hours as I expected, I actually had to call Susan within a few hours. I walked around the house repeating "this feels different" over and over again. Paul attempted to comfort me that "different" was what I had been working for. "Different" might be just what I was dreaming about. Different might mean that these contractions were actually effective. Perhaps, and I feared to even consider it, just perhaps I was dilating.

Susan was at the house by five, called Rebecca, and we called my aunt to come sit with Joey. And this time my water broke in a sweeping gush just like in the movies. We arrived at the hospital before seven and I think they checked me. I think I was in transition. I think I was fully in my body and birthing. Just birthing. On my knees and on my back and in the hall and with noise and with Susan and Paul and Rebecca all holding me up. I remember that Susan told the grumpy nurse that she should go take a short break, that we didn't need her. I remember that this meant that this was it. I was doing this part, but I had never gotten to this part before. There was something else that needed to happen.

I was on my knees, holding on to the top of the bed and rocking and Rebecca put her face next to mine and whispered in my ear, "I'm going to give you a couple of minutes to figure this out and then I'll have to tell you what to do." I have no idea what she really said. I don't have any idea what the hell that even means. It worked. It shifted. I was worried that she was going to take over and I got it. Oh, pushing. That was what happened next. Pushing.

I grabbed pushing with every ounce of my being and I shot that beautiful boy straight out in a roar of power that I did not know I had. I pushed while she said things that I didn't hear. I think she wanted me to slow down, but just a bit. She wanted me to let him do some of the work. She wanted to give me time to open and stretch and work with my baby. I heard and felt nothing but heat and joy and movement, movement that had never happened before.

Wet, slippery, naked baby landed in Rebecca's hands with Paul over her shoulder and Susan over mine and the grumpy nurse on a coffee break. Just us. And he came to my arms, which were free of tubes and needles and I lifted him to my chest and I cried and I released my trauma again. I knew it was something different than I had ever known or ever considered, but maybe it was just what I had always known and always considered. Maybe I had always known that this was birth. Maybe somehow I had known for 20 years that birth should and could be this.

My tiny "premature" 37-week baby weighed in at nine pounds, eight ounces. He held his head up and turned to look at the doctor when he came to check him out. And he nursed. I had believed for 20 years that my less-than-adequate breasts had not only made me uncomfortable all through high school, they were also unable to produce enough milk to feed my own child. I had believed I might be able to birth naturally, but I had actually never considered that I was also capable of nursing successfully. Somehow no one ever explained to me that recovering from surgery while trying to establish nursing was hard. I had left the hospital the first time with Nate on formula carrying that lovely gift pack from the formula company. He hated nursing and I fought hard to nurse him about half of the time for about nine months, which I am really proud of. With Joey they only "allowed" me to leave the hospital with supplemental formula and check in with his doctor. They were worried about him. He had lost a lot of weight. (Seriously people. Babies lose about 10% of their birth weight. Why don't they tell mommas that? And a couple of ounces doesn't seem like a lot, but my boys weighed over 10 pounds—you do the math.) Joey had jaundice. All of this was somehow my failure and frightening, rather than expected given our surgical birth experience. Zach nursed like a champ but more importantly, I could keep up with him and we went home strong and with no concerns.

Zach left the hospital less than 48 hours later. Oh, I tore a ton. I didn't hear the slow down stuff. I don't actually recommend shooting a nearly 10 pound baby out of your vagina, at least not at high speed. Zach was perfect. I was higher than a kite. Rebecca admitted in the moments following the birth that she didn't really think I could do it. But that was OK. Think what she might, she never let me know that she had doubts. She gave me the chance and I ran with it. I knew myself differently. I knew I could and I had and it was over. And of course once again the baby was fine and so was I and a beautiful birth stays with you just as powerfully and just as long as a rough one does. It follows you like a gift and a blessing.

My boys know the stories of their births. Not so much the yucky stuff. I tell them each tenderly. When Zach was four, I was involved in the natural birth world and we actually marched on our state capital for safe birth options. He told a friend of ours that he was the first one of my kids to find the hole. Kids are pretty amazing. Who knows what he knows. He says his brothers got distracted and didn't do their work, it kind of fits.

The birth psychology people say that babies born surgically have a ton of faith, warranted or not, that someone will always come and rescue them. Zach got pushed out early, on my schedule, and he is a take charge guy with a bit of a chip on his shoulder. I haven't been able to take control of Zach, but at least he cooperated with my birth plan and he's kind of proud of that.

Chapter 19
Heads Up!

by Adrienne C Caldwell Bodyworker & Teacher

Everyone I know, knows I have been working on this book for years. Lots of people offered me their stories. When I started, birth trauma stories were hard to find. I am so thrilled that the whole range of birth stories, not just the bragging one, are getting easier for people to find. I will share just a couple and then I ask you to consider sharing yours on my website or FB page.

Since these are not mine to tell.. they are written and shared just as they were shared with me. (Including the amazing testimonials.)

Maureen

My husband and I were so excited to have our first baby. We prepared for a home birth with our midwife - Rachael McGraw, went to birth classes, started to acquire all sorts of baby do-dads, then...baby is breech at week 33, still at 35, still at 37. We tried Chiropractic Webster's technique, acupuncture, moxibustion, inversions, headphones on the lower part of the belly, ice at the top of the uterus and heat at the bottom - yup, this baby really

191

didn't want to turn. This is when our midwife referred us to Gail Tully of Spinning Babies. Gail confirmed the baby's position and referred us to Dennis Hartung, OB, to begin preparations for a possible hospital birth. We did attempt an external cephalic version with Dr. Hartung - Doc tries to turn baby manually while you are hooked up to all sorts of monitors. I still had a dream of having baby at home but baby had different plans. I was scheduled for induction on the morning of September 23 in Hudson. I feel fortunate that labor started spontaneously at 559 am, alarm was set for 600 am.

Husband becomes a Hero

We drove to Hudson, the dashboard makes a great doula for sacral pressure in the car! My water broke in the car, too - oh joy! We labored all day surrounded by our amazing team of midwives - Rachel McGraw, Gail Tully, and Karen Garley, our doula - Vanessa Wilcox, Dr. Hartung, and his nurses. Bruce, my husband, was my main support and hero of the day. He held me up, watched me expel more fluids than he thought the human body had, and had a silly joke around every corner. Plus he played the banjo - how many gals are lucky enough to have live music at their labor? I laughed through my contractions. I was so overjoyed to know my body had started labor on its own. Of course, as contractions became more intense I had to laugh between contractions.

Once I was checked, which Denny did not do until well into active labor, I began to dissociate - I am a survivor of sexual assault and rape. I neglected to inform him of this detail. As a result, it has taken three years for me to begin to regain memory of active labor and birth. As an aside, please, if you are a survivor, inform your providers. It does matter and it will make a difference for your labor and birth experience.

Anyway, I know we worked pretty hard through the late afternoon and into the evening. All day long Bruce was by my side and holding me up. We were slow dancing, working with the rebozo, hanging out in the shower, walking about, hands and knees, lunging, hanging from the birth bar - I think we tried everything to get that baby to come on down. We did get to pushing and the pain was too intense, the checks were excruciating, and everyone was beginning to feel a little discouraged. Baby was doing well - the monitor showed baby was well and bearing with us. We were given the choice of cesarean or epidural. I had an irrational fear of cesarean, so we went with the epidural. Being a redhead, I don't respond to analgesics well.

I passed out. My team called me back. I couldn't move. I had the skin crawls and itch that makes you want to rip your skin off. And I had a really hard time focusing. I was on my back, exactly where I really didn't want to give birth. I was hoping to use gravity. I have finally remembered that I had a midwife on each leg, Vanessa and Bruce at my head, and Denny and Gail on the business end of birth. I can remember feeling Denny slowly working baby down. Her feet were out! I reached down and felt them. Time to go back to work. Her hips and shoulders were out - with help from Denny. And then I heard Rachael yell PUSH! Rachael doesn't yell, ever, so I pushed and baby was born. I have a physical memory of pushing baby's head out but I feel like I may still be forgetting something. I do remember not hearing her cry right away. This scared me and I kept asking about her and then I finally heard the most beautiful cry on earth. After that cry my memory is very poor. I know there are details of the final minutes of baby's birth that I don't remember.

It's a girl! I named her Magnolia Rose. She was rushed to the pediatricians. Her APGAR was 3 - 5- 7. She seemed to be doing alright and then she crashed. Full organ and brain failure, possible seizures, everything that could go wrong did go wrong and she was rushed to Children's in St. Paul. At the time I was unaware of how serious things were. We stayed in Hudson until we received a call from St. Paul saying we needed to come because she might not make it much longer. We were floored, and made the worlds fastest trip from Hudson to St. Paul. Then our journey really began.

A Different Road

Magnolia was put on a cooling bed for three days as soon as she was admitted to Children's. We were uncertain and completely in the dark about the treatments being done and what they meant, other than what the neonatologists told us. We were fortunate to have a very kind staff who was willing to indulge my over inquisitive mind and help us get through our experience as well as possible. There were some extremely difficult decisions made during our stay in the NICU. I had to become an advocate for myself and learn not to listen to the rhetoric from the neonatologists that my daughter was the way she was because I bore her vaginally. I began to really learn about how special breech babies are and what they can teach us. We had so much support, from everywhere. The support and love was a welcome form of feeling overwhelmed.

Every day Bruce played banjo and read stories to Magnolia while we were in the hospital. After two weeks we were able to breathe a little easier - Magnolia was going to make it. We were told at that point that she was going to be severely disabled. Another hurdle. Me being me, I put the pressure on to up our complementary care. Daily, I did reflexology for her. Twice a week she received Healing Touch and CranioSacral therapy. I did reflexology on her everyday. I applied breast milk to the reflex areas that corresponded with whatever area of her body needed the extra help. Every time she had a session, her numbers improved the next morning. We kept it up the entire stay and she continues to get complementary care today. By the time we were discharged her status was upped to being moderately disabled. After a couple years of special ed., and more bodywork (chiropractic, craniosacral, massage, yoga, reflexology, and myofascial release) - she is so wonderfully normal! Beautifully sassy and doing everything a three-year-old should.

Revelations of a Breech

Also, as far as I know, and I have asked, there are no more breech deliveries with mamas on their back in Hudson. Everyone is on hands and knees - unpublished studies have shown this is the best position for mama and baby (Frankfurt studies). I have also learned since, that the treatable disability my daughter has most likely developed in utero and did not occur as a result of her birth - in fact, the literature says her disability is one the most common reasons babies are breech, in the first place.

I am growing out of my grief and becoming more of a geek than I already was, and working at being the best mama I can to a very special little lady.

As a result I have turned my career as an educator and bodyworker to helping women and families know about breech birth. I feel like I do my best work in therapy room helping moms with sore body's and restricted spaces. Magnolia has given me so many gifts I can never repay her for - She is a bright light in my world and the inspiration for so much that I do.

Mother's Guilt & Recovery

After the intensity of the first 6 months of having a special needs baby I came to realization that I desperately needed to return to counseling. I had already been in the great care of Maureen Campion before Magnolia's birth to try and work through issues of rape, sexual assault, and abuse. After meeting with Maureen and my doula I realized that I had been dissociated for a good portion of the last part of my labor due to being checked for dilation. The checks were done by a very kind, very gentle Dr. Hartung but he is a he and my body did not recognize the difference between him and my past assailants. That was a startling revelation. I believe I met weekly after M's birth for quite a while with Maureen to try and reconcile the decisions that I made during my pregnancy and labor. Please know, I would not change a thing. I discovered I have a pathological fear of being cut on the abdomen and was suffering the effects of PTSD. Every day for a long time I had vivid dreams of atrocities being committed to my child, I heard crying babies every moment I was not touching her, I had visions of mangled baby in the depths of sleepless nights. As I write this it is amazing to me that I did not completely lose my mind. As well as the PTSD I deal with the grief of not getting the peaceful home birth I had prepared so carefully for with my husband and birth team. It had turned into a 3 ring circus, complete with the tent collapsing at the end of the show. As time healed me, my community held me up, my husband muddled through, and we started feeling well enough to discuss having a second baby. We immediately knew it was the right thing to do for us and for our daughter. She had graduated from her Special Ed services and was being declared healthy by all of her docs. So now, a sibling. And now, how do we make the best decisions for this pregnancy and baby. Maureen helped me feel okay about changing my birth team with exception to Dr. Hartung. Bruce & I knew he was the only OB we would be comfortable with for having as natural a birth experience as possible in a hospital setting. We hired a well experienced doula, changed chiropractors, kept up with counseling to dispel fears and anxiety, and got regular massage. Now the only thing I was obsessive about with my second pregnancy was baby positioning. Big shocker! I pretty much stalked Gail Tully for my entire 9 months learning, and begging for confirmation of a head down babe. She was so gracious to oblige. Baby boy was head down throughout the entire pregnancy but was also posterior - direct OP (for the geeks out there). This did give me a little more anxiety than I would have like but he was head down, I had already gotten a footling breech out of my pelvis, and oh the hours and hours of yoga and squats. My labor for #2 was fast, he did finally turn about 2 hours into a 5 hour labor. He was peacefully born into the water on June 20 in the early morning. My heart and soul were healed in the moment he slid into the water and opened his arms and eyes. I honestly feel that my birth would not have been that profoundly healing if I had not been getting regular counseling from Maureen. Discussing fears, guilt, shame, and all the other emotions that go with living life is very helpful before you embark on the journey of labor and birth. It is my humble opinion that if you have lived any moment of trauma in your life a good counselor is worth her weight in gold in helping you prepare for labor and birth.

Chapter 20
Cori's Story

by Cori Wallace

To fully understand the impact that the birth of my fourth had on me, I need to preface this story with the descriptions of my two previous births.

My first daughter was born via cesarean section after 56 hours of labor and 3 ½ hours of pushing. I was 19 years old and very misinformed regarding most aspects of birth. After pushing for over three hours, I was transferred from the care of my midwife to an OB and was quickly coerced into accepting a non-emergent cesarean section for failure to progress. I was made to feel that my body would never be able to birth a baby. I was inadequate, bad at birth. Something I was born to do, and I sucked at it; that is pretty much what I took from my first birth. I left the hospital happy that I had a healthy baby but completely devastated and in pain. I also left with a drive to learn everything possible about birth and how to avoid this from happening to me and to people I knew again.

My husband and I wanted our children close in age. After 16 months of trying to conceive, I scheduled an appointment with my long time gynecologist. I was given the lowest dose of a fertility drug called Clomid. It was miserable. I hated life while taking Clomid. After the first cycle I swore that I could never take it again, even if it meant never having another child. A few weeks later, I saw those beautiful two pink lines and was relieved that I would never have to touch Clomid again!

Shortly after getting a "BFP," of Big Fat Positive, as it is commonly referred to on forums and parenting boards, I started spotting. Fearing the worst, I quickly went to my urgent care and they decided that a blood test that day and another in two days would be the most accurate measurement of a viable pregnancy. When I got my results back, my HcG levels were through the roof, and after a few hours scouring the internet for information on "High HcG levels," I was convinced I was having more than one baby! Of course the rest of the world thought I was just an over excited young mom looking for attention.

After meeting with my midwife and explaining my thoughts regarding a multiple pregnancy, she happily set me up for a dating ultrasound to get an accurate due date. I clearly remember telling the ultrasound technician that she would be seeing two yolk sacs during the ultrasound, and she reassured me that it was normal to think that there were twins because pregnancy was simply more than most people could stand, especially a young mom, like me. Within 7 seconds of her placing the probe to my abdomen, I saw the two sacs and loudly yelled, "I told you so." Score one point for my momma intuition!

I had a very uneventful pregnancy. I started seeing an OB and planned a VBAC (vaginal birth after a cesarean) at St. John's Hospital in Maplewood. My previous midwife did not see VBAC patients. My OB was comfortable with my birth plan and I was determined to have a natural birth! I remember going to my 28 week appointment. During the routine ultrasound, it was found that my cervix was funneling at both ends and was significantly shorter than what it should be for any pregnancy at 28 weeks, regardless of how many babies I was carrying. I was given my first round of steroid shots to strengthen my babies' lungs, should my cervix not hold and was put on very strict bed rest. I woke up the next morning in active labor and rushed to the hospital. Due to extenuating medical circumstances, an emergency cesarean was called and I gave birth to a 2lb 12oz baby boy and a 2lb 10oz baby girl.

I did not deal with the same anxiety I had about my first birth. I went into this pregnancy prepared and felt good about all of the decisions that were made. Obviously I had hoped for a full term natural delivery, but given the circumstances, I was just happy to have both of my babies. I knew that I did everything I could to prevent unnecessary interventions. I was not sad the same way that I was after my first.

After sixty-one days in the NICU, my babies were both finally at home and the last thing on my mind was further adding to our family. I was wrapped up in feeding schedules and diaper changes. My babies were not healthy and we were seeing specialists on a weekly basis. No more than 4 months after my babies had been discharged from the NICU, my husband and I were shocked by the previously welcomed two pink lines. I cannot honestly say that I was even excited. I was already dealing with the loss of normalcy and the chaos that prematurity brings to your life, I couldn't fathom another human being to be responsible for.

After coming to grips that I'd soon have three babies, ages fourteen months and younger and a preschooler, I started looking into the logistics of my next birth. My previous OB declared that I would not be a candidate for a VBAC after two cesareans. I interviewed a handful of OB's and midwives. No one was able to commit to me. I was too high risk. I felt hopeless and out of good options, until I came across Vanessa.

Her name was the last on my list of people to call and I cannot be more thankful that I did! She is a VBAC mom herself and truly has faith in the bodies of women. She took us on and I breathed a sigh of relief. I might still get that chance to birth a baby the way I was made to.

This pregnancy was not as easy as the last. Yes, my twin pregnancy was easier than this one. I fully believe that it was mostly psychological. I was nervous, scared and stressed. I had a bout of threatened pre-term labor around the same gestation that my twins were born. I was reassured by Vanessa that I was not at a huge risk for another preterm delivery and that I was capable of carrying this baby to full term. It was very comforting to hear this.

As she predicted, my due date not only came, but it went. I joked that I was gestating longer to make up for the shortened pregnancy with my twins. I was ten days past my due date, had surrendered to the length of the pregnancy, and was comfortable with letting my baby decide when to be born. I went to bed early that night. It just a few minutes before 1:00 a.m. and I was roused from sleep by the deepest twisting surge. I woke my husband and joked that he would not be going to work the next day. I went to the bathroom, assuming that my full bladder had played a role in my discomfort, and returned to my bed to sleep. It was no more than twelve minutes later, I was awoken again by the same feeling. It was no longer comfortable to lie down. I sat up in bed, watched my husband try and catch a few more minutes of sleep and picked up a word search to pass the time. The next few rushes started coming closer and closer together. It was silly to think that I had planned on doing a word search. By the time they were 6 minutes apart I asked my husband to call Vanessa. It was 2:00am. Lance filled the tub and I was relieved to have the water supporting my body, but things were still very intense.

The midwife arrived at 3:15 a.m. I was still in the tub, focusing on squatting and letting my pelvis open, but the contractions were close together and not lasting more than 20-30 seconds. I requested to be checked, something my midwife did not routinely do. I was absolutely devastated to find that my cervix was still high. So high, in fact, the midwife could not even reach it. This meant that I was not dilated or effaced. This, combined with the nature of my contractions meant that I likely had an occiput posterior baby, the cause for my prolonged labor the first time around.

With my oldest, I was already dilated 5 centimeters when I arrived at the hospital and they broke my water. It wasn't disclosed until after she was born surgically, but when they had ruptured my bags, the rush of water had lodged her into an unnatural position. She was sunny side up and her chin was not tucked. Had I left well alone, she would have stood a chance. My body would have done what it was supposed to. Because of that simple rupture the midwife did to supposedly speed things along, my labor stopped, was restarted with artificial oxytocin which created unnaturally strong contractions which cleared the path to an epidural. This is what I have come refer to as the downward spiral of medical interventions. It is all too common.

Back to my labor at home; Vanessa recommended that I do an inversion to give my baby a chance to come out of the pelvic bones and re-situate in a better position. We moved to the bedroom and I laid there with my hips high in the air and my chest pressed to the bed. She recommended an hour in this position. After four rushes there, I couldn't stay. I needed to move and be upright. I was angry and in pain. Being frustrated during labor is one of the worst things! I know why Vanessa doesn't give vaginal exams to women during labor- it's usually going to be a letdown if you solely base your progress off of centimeters dilated. There are so many other factors. I decided to move to my bathroom and sit on the toilet. I needed to pee anyways and I knew it was a good position for opening my pelvis. I also knew that I could get some privacy by simply shutting the door.

My spirit broke while I was sitting in there. I started asking for the logistics of getting to the hospital and Lance and Vanessa happily obliged. It was my choice, and I knew that, but I think I was looking more for reassurance and guidance rather than a ride to the hospital. I continued to sit on the toilet between rushes and stand and dance with my bathroom door during them. I thought of my dear friend Shana, who talks about dancing with her lamp during her labor at home. It worked for her and it worked for me. I swayed my hips, rolled from my heels to the balls of my feet and back down again. Lance came to check on me and was shocked by the amount of blood in the toilet. I looked and sure enough, I had finally lost my plug. I thought back to the last few contractions and noticed that they were feeling much more productive. I was getting rests between them, too, which was vital to my mental health.

I started feeling hot and sweaty and wanted to get in the shower. I loved the cold sting my shower walls gave my back and used that to get through the next few rushes. I continued this way for a few more rushes and was caught off guard by a severe pain in my tailbone. My thoughts were that the baby had rotated again and was now in a bad position again. I rushed out of the shower and down the stairs. I think I had intentions of yelling at my midwife about how the inversion hadn't worked and that the baby was going to be stuck forever. I had no idea that by the time I one leg lifted over the edge of the birth pool, my whole body would start pushing. It was not a conscious effort. It was something I had no control over. Since I had labored so privately, and had not kept my husband or midwife in the loop about my tail bone pains, which were actually the baby descending into the birth canal, no one expected me to actually be through transition. The apprentice started making the compresses and tea for my postpartum and the midwife gathered her supplies to have on hand. I reached down to support my skin as it stretched and felt the fleshy wrinkles of her head and the wispy down that she had for hair. It was at that point that I regained faith in my body to birth this baby.

Vanessa checked for heart tones as I fought her off. I was so wrapped up in getting this baby out and the sensation of being touched made my skin burn. My nerves were on fire throughout my entire body. I forcefully pushed and her head was born. I should have listened to Vanessa about easing her head out, but I was not able to regulate the pushing. I had little control over my body at this point. While still in the water, I rotated to a hands and knees position and Vanessa supported the baby as she was born. She passed her back through my legs and I came to a kneeling position. I saw her under the water and a surge of hormones took over. I was overcome with love and pride for this baby, the birth, my support team and my family. I lifted her out, confirmed that she was indeed a girl and waited for her to breathe. She took her time and eventually needed some light suction from the nasal aspirator. She perked up and cried. After 20 minutes of letting her get the important blood from my placenta, we clamped and cut the cord. Vanessa handed her to Lance and she lay on his chest, taking in his scent and voice.

I was still waiting for my placenta to detach. I moved to the bathroom again and was finally able to birth the placenta just over 40 minutes after Audry was born. Vanessa made a print from my placenta, something that was important for me to have. It made a beautiful shape. It was her tree of life. When I look at the print, I am reminded of how birth has shaped my life. It was before 6:00a.m. I was shocked to learn that the entire ordeal took just smidge longer than five hours.

I had lost faith in what my body was capable of doing. I had just about surrendered to the idea that I was just broken and inadequate. Birthing Audry has made a huge impact on my self image and confidence. I have renewed faith! After my first was born, I was on a mission to learn everything I could about birth and how to avoid others from having the same situation. I took doula courses, learned about pregnancy health and nutrition and devoted many hours to being available to pregnant women and sharing what I'd learned. I am a part time doula/pregnancy coach with a passion for natural birth. I would love to learn traditional midwifery in the future. I have found that there is an enormous lack of informed consent when it comes to medical interventions and birth. To anyone who is reading this and is expecting; I challenge you to take charge of your birth! Learn all of your options and build a support team of people who believe in you. If it hadn't been for the support of my husband, Lance, or my amazing midwife, Vanessa Stephens Coldwater of Family Tree Midwifery, who knows how my third birth would have turned out. To be honest, I don't care to even think about it. I'd rather spend my time educating others to make educated choices for their births so that they are not faced with the same challenges I was.

Cori's story can be found on the All Things Diapers blog.

http://allthingsdiapers.blogspot.com/search?updated-max=2012-01-01T00%3A01%3A00-06%3A00&max-results=1

Chapter 21
Sam and Sarah Saying Hello and Goodbye

by Catie HyungJu Equality Chi

Infant loss cesarean

Author's note: Because I wanted this to be as honest and full an account of my twins, everything is in here. Sometimes I swore like a sailor, some of my thoughts were not beautiful, and I just wanted to let you know before you got too far. Thank you for reading this, and I hope something here helps you.

The Early Days

On Valentine's Day, the day before our daughter Emma's fifth birthday, we found out we were pregnant again. Although I had only had a little spotting in January, I thought this was due to the stress. I sat in the doctor's office, staring at the "+" sign while Emma called Mike at work and told him the news. By the end of the month, we knew it was twins. My father died in early March and I was convinced that the twins were my reward; a balance for the sadness of my father's long death from an Alzheimer's related disease.

210

Since I was now a full-time diabetic, we accepted our OB's advice about having an amniocentesis performed on the twins. By the end of April, I knew I was carrying a boy and a girl, both genetically perfect. Then, on May 13, I went in for a Level 2 ultrasound that I considered routine. I didn't even bring Mike with, since what could possibly be wrong? The sonographer asked me some strange questions - "Did you have these twins by in-vitro?", "Do you have other children at home?" Looking back, I can see that these were questions to prepare me for Sarah's death. She said she could only find one heartbeat and then the doctor came in and I heard the words, "The female is dead."

As the words sank in, I could only babble for my husband. The doctor said something about how it was not important that I call him, because he couldn't get there before the Level 2 was over. I remember swearing at the tech to get me a fucking phone. The doctor told me that we still had one baby and implied that if I didn't calm down, something would happen to my boy. That shut me up while they went in search of the woman in charge of pregnancy loss. I must have gotten dressed, because I had to have been partially naked for the ultrasound. They sent me to a room with a phone and I called Mike, then my mom and a bunch of friends.

After Mike got there, I really wanted to get back home. I couldn't think of how to tell our five year old daughter, who had been joyfully kissing my belly and hoping for a sister. We had only just told her that she was definitely going to have a sister a few weeks before. How could we take away the gift she had so much wanted and we had already thought we had given to her? We had just picked out names and I had decided on the babies' sweater patterns for my mother-in-law to knit. By instinct alone, we sat Emma between us and gently told her that her sister was already dead. Her response was the honest feeling of a sister already provoked by a three year old brother - "I wish the boy had died." She asked if she could tell her Mike's parents and her uncles, which we allowed since she wanted to and neither of us were up to it.

Surviving

After Sarah died, nothing was the same. Some days, I was a zombie and on others I worked on my community playground project. Physically, I felt much better - but then I felt horrible about feeling better. Emotionally, I felt I had failed everyone I wanted to make happy; Mike would have loved another little girl. My mom had retired to help me out when the twins got here. After we got the amnio back, I told everyone. Now I had to tell them again. This seemed to me to be the hardest stage and it didn't help that my husband's sister-in-law told some people in my neighborhood without asking me if she should. So I never knew who knew what and I never knew when someone was going to come up and tell me how sorry they were. One time, it was just at the first moment I could remember NOT thinking about Sarah when someone told me how sorry they were. This sister-in-law kept telling me she knew "exactly" how I felt until I nearly screamed, "How long did you have to carry around the dead and rotting body of your child!"

I could never escape my sorrow and pretend that life was normal. One day, at the grocery store, I heard the clerk telling the person behind me my story. Great, I thought, I am going to be everyone's "I heard of a woman who had to carry a live twin and a dead twin." People with the best of intentions said the most horrible things. Oddly, I couldn't even bear strangers not knowing about Sarah, so when I received the passing questions and congratulations about my growing belly, I still told almost everyone that I was carrying two babies. I would try and NOT tell people, but it would always surface. I would feel my face twist into a tight and awkward position, to help keep me from crying right then and there, and then the twins' story would tumble out.

One of the things that saved my mind during this time was working on the playground at the school by my home. This school is a third Hispanic, mostly industrial migrant workers, a third African-American, and a third whatever else we all are. Over 75% of the kids qualify for the free/reduced federal lunch program. I have spent a year and half doing everything from coordinating tools to all the public relations. Sam and Sarah's original due date was August 15th. That weekend, over 200 parents and neighbors installed the play equipment, which I helped design and select. The thought that I was working on this playground that one of my children would never see was too much, until some neighbors gave me a gift of a tree for her memory and said I could plant it wherever I wanted to. Emma, Jake and Sam will be shaded by their sister's burr oak tree, which will stand alone in the native grasses garden.

Mostly, survival for me took the form of counting down the days and then the hours until it would all be over. At least, I thought it would all be over.

The Birth

My OB advised a Cesarean delivery because that would be the only way we might get answers to what had caused Sarah's death. One of her partners, who had done our twins' amnio, had also done a great deal of research into placental implantation and abnormalities. I wrote a birth plan, made a bunch of copies for all the nurses.

The first date for the twins was the 25th, but that changed to the 23rd to accommodate the second OB's schedule; delivering two days sooner seemed like a blessing. I was very nervous, but decided to work myself into a state of exhaustion by planning a little get together for five hundred people on the evening before. It was the dedication ceremony for the playground. I was tired and barely packed for the operation. We had to be there at 5:30 without eating or drinking anything since midnight. My mom sacked out on the couch and quietly wished the best for us as we left.

The anesthesiologist was very competent and supported my decision for an epidural, although he did seem to favor a spinal. My choice was based on the emergency cesarean births of my first two children. This time, something went wrong and I started to feel the knife halfway through the procedure. Nothing helped - not even the nitrous oxide. I vaguely remember saying something about feeling like goddamn Jane Seymour, but I may have only thought it. Finally, my OB asked me if I had had enough and I said yes. (One incredibly ignorant person asked me how I knew that the epidural hadn't worked. Answer: Because I was screaming). I will never forget the concern and fear on Mike's face. Also, this was a freakish occurrence and very rare.

The pain was something I am trying to forget, but the general anesthesia was a blessing. When the sterile field screen was lowered, I started thinking about how Sarah was finally going to be leaving the one and only place she had ever been held, or ever would be held. After this, she would be on her way to becoming ashes; a dream that was not to be, a sadness that would never heal completely. I said the Buddhist mantra, which helped, but could not take away the pain. I was happy to go under.

The first words I can now remember hearing were from my OB. "Sarah is right here when you are ready to see her, or you can let the staff know." Supposedly, I looked awake for awhile before anything registered. I looked at Mike and he was holding a dark-haired baby with shiny black button eyes. This was Samuel Thomas. He was the most beautiful thing I had ever seen.

Still groggy, I got to hold Sam as we were wheeled to what would be our room for the next few days. My nurse was Myrna Lou, who could not have been gentler; she got a hand print from Sarah for us to keep. There was a picture of a leaf with dew on it on the door to our room, signifying that we had lost our baby. The hospital provided a Polaroid and a camera loaded with black and white film, as well as a professional photo of Sarah for us. We have the Polaroids, but they allow grieving parents a bit of space to ask for the rest of the pictures.

Sam was amazing. Born at 8:40 AM, weighing seven pounds, ten ounces and 20.5 inches with 8/10 APGARs. At first he seemed so tiny, until I remembered he had just been inside of me. Then he seemed huge. He nursed easily and right away - I could have attached him to my nipple and not even held him (of course I did). In fact, I dozed while nursing him when he hadn't had the nipple all the way in his mouth and he actually gave me a blister! Emma had a little bit of peach-colored fuzz when she was born; Jake hardly had hair until he was two. It gave me so much pleasure to watch Mike hold him so carefully, even though this child did not look so much like him. I don't know why this strikes me, since I love all my children. I had assumed that there would never be a child that looked like me. Wisdom and understanding shone through his blue-black eyes; he seemed to be telling me that the sorrow we had shared inside my body was only the beginning. It would not always be sorrow - we would be promising each other a measure of joy in the rest of our love.

Settled in, I asked for the basket my mother made to hold Sarah. She was not what you would call beautiful, although at 18 centimeters, she was a good deal longer than I expected. When I first saw her, I thought that she had been flattened out in profile, but before she left us forever, I looked at her in the sunlight and what I had thought was her nose was really her ear. You could make out the tiny slits which might have been eyes as beautiful as Emma's. Sarah definitely had her sister's stubborn chin. Only one hand still looked like very much like a hand and her feet were pretty much gone. The attitude her body was in reminded me of old paintings of the dead Jesus Christ being taken down from the cross, but I still hoped that her death was peaceful. I stroked her head and felt her cranium, wondering what mysteries she held there and if she knew she was alive. For some reason, I felt her neck and the rest of her body. I guess I have always been a great neck nuzzler, but when I touched her throat, a tiny moan came out. I don't even know how there could have been a sound in her, she was so tiny and fragile. I know I will hear the echo of this sound, for the rest of my life, in everything remotely like it. Already Jake has played on a toy clarinet and my heart stopped for a minute, taking a tiny detour into my throat. The only thing I could say, to myself and beneath my breath, was, "She was real."

The only tough part about my stay, besides walking again, was one nurse whose name I have blissfully forgotten. First, she bottle fed Sam without asking me, then she gave him formula instead of sugar water. She was just so convinced that Sam was losing weight because he was not nursing correctly even though I kept saying, "Could it be because my milk isn't in?" After Emma and Jake were there for a visit, she started mewling, "You are going to be SO busy." I finally said, "You know, I was planning on being a lot busier, so could you not say that." I couldn't believe it, usually I am only brave after the fight (or my flight) is over. Maybe this is Sarah's legacy to me.

Early on, I had wanted Mike to be able to say that he would wash Sarah and take care of her for me while I was recovering. Because he is both more laid back then I am and also because he did not feel a pressing need to bathe her, he could not guarantee his actions. He wanted to see how she was before he made up his mind. After a lot of fighting and many bitter words, the light dawned on me that this was not ONLY my loss, but Mike's and our family's sadness as well. When I finally began to imagine how this day would go, I could have written out contingencies for every possibility until my birth plan looked like a critical path analysis. Mike was content that we would cross each bridge together and that we had surrounded ourselves with people who would give us the best guidance.

One of the most painful decisions was to negotiate with ourselves what we thought was best for our two other kids. We decided to start with Polaroids of Sarah for each of the children and watch their reactions to see what to do next. Jake, who turned three last March, glanced at his picture and was, as expected, not very interested. Emma looked at her picture and wanted to see her sister. Carefully, and with what can only be described as reverence, she held the basket that contained her sister's body. She would hold the coverlet tenderly in her hands and with her whole heart in her face, she would help us decorate her basket with flowers from the bouquets we received. I brought four gift enclosure cards, one for each of us, and we each wrote a little something and tucked into her basket. Emma bravely asked if she could carry her sister to the lady from the Cremation Society, which she did. The woman tucked her in tenderly; the small Madeline doll was much bigger than Sarah and a little unwieldy.

I had really thought that once Sam was in my arms and Sarah was gone, my grief would be less. He is here and with me and I feel that we share something beyond just my carrying him inside me. As someone wise and kind said, "At least Sarah wasn't alone when she died." This has been of great comfort to me. I also went to the Pregnancy and Infant Loss Center's annual remembrance day on Sunday. I was doing all right - some tears, but Sam tooted along every once in a while, making me giggle that embarrassed giggle we all once had. Then they handed out plants to each family that had experienced a loss. I went to get our plants, carrying Sam, proud of him, but worried that the sight of him might make others feel more sad. As I carried my plant back, the thought struck me that this plant tucked into the crook of my arm was taking my Sarah's place. She should have been there. There are no plants beautiful, magical and wonderful enough to bring her back or to replace her.

When I started this tome many days ago, I was hoping that the writing of it would bring me clarity and some sort of closure. I had thought that saying goodbye to Sarah in the hospital would be enough for me. What I can see now is that this sorrow will be part of me that will never be lost ~ both because I can't forget my daughter. Also, because I don't want even want to try. Someone somewhere wrote that, over time, our losses become a shaded thread in the tapestry that is our lives. A blessing from my heart to yours.

Catie

Chapter 22
The Story of Little Man

by Sara Johnson-Steffey

My body was contracting for a week before you came. I spent hours pacing the floors of the house, literally wringing my hands, and crying.

Was this supposed to happen?

We went to the hospital late one night. I was 1cm dilated. The nurses laughed and sent me home. I was so mad no one was taking me seriously. THIS IS REAL! I wanted to yell at them.

The next day I decided to smile through the pain, not let it get to me. We went to the park, next to the rose garden by the lake. Your dada laid out a blanket. Sitting under the crabapple trees, shaded from the summer heat, I finally felt at peace with you coming, the not knowing of it all.

My giant belly, with you squirming inside, was so uncomfortable in the heat but, I was at peace. We ate grapes and salads from the deli and talked and laughed. I laid with my head in your ada's lap, squinting up at the blue sky, sunlight dancing through the leaves.

At 2am that night my water broke.

I was ready.

We went to the hospital. The same nurses let us in this time. I refused drugs for hours. I wanted you born under the best possible circumstances. Finally I relented, just to take the edge off they told me. I rolled on a ball, listening to music through my ipod, the same ipod that saw me through flight after flight into Baghdad, runs in the dusty heat. This time I, as a warrior, focused in on the music, each wave of pain rolling through me, requiring concentration I didn't know I had.

But you wouldn't come.

They told me you were stuck, your little head tilted to the side, and your heart rate was dipping. I didn't know then but that was pretty normal at 7 cm and in transition. I learned later that if I had gotten up, walked around, moved a little you would've likely un-stuck yourself.

But, I didn't know. I was scared and tired. I took the epidural. They gave me 30 minutes of lying on my side to "see if that helps."

When they came back they told me you would have to be cut out of my belly. I was devastated. I sobbed and sobbed. Please, isn't there any other way? I wanted this to be perfect, your entrance into the world. I should've fought back but I didnt know.

Resigned to what they told us, they wheeled me into the sterile room. I was exhausted from 16 hours of struggle, plus the days before of pre-labor. The doctors worked for an hour to un-wedge you out of my pelvis. I choked on my vomit, neon green stomach bile, and lurched to the side. They yelled at me to be still. I focused my breathing, again, for you, taking tiny gasps of air so they could get you out.

Finally they pulled you from me, and cut the cord that attached us together for so long. I felt suddenly empty, like part of me had been removed. But then they held your wriggling red and bruised body over the curtain so I could see you.

My boy. My son. My Jack.

They took you to the table to check you out. I wanted desperately to hold you, touch you, but I was too tired to insist. Your squall sounded so scared, almost frantic. I could see you on the little table right by my head. Dada crying tears of joys over you.

I called out in a croaking voice, "It's okay, little man. Mama is here. I am here!"

You immediately stopped crying and turned your head toward me.

And in that instant I fell in love. We were no longer one, but you were mine.

Chapter 23
Anonymous

Five years ago I was pregnant with my first child. I was excited and happy to be starting a family. I always wanted children. All the women in my family have very easy pregnancies and labor. I thought I would have the same luck. I was not as fortunate. I developed pre-eclampsia at 30 weeks which was the beginning of a highly medicalized birth. At 36 weeks, I was induced due to severe pre-eclampsia, my internal organs were starting to fail. Within 10 hours I was fully dialed and started to push. After 4 ½ hours of no progress and continued increases in my blood pressure, the doctor told me I needed a cesarean. I was too tired to care at the point, I just wanted to see my baby.

During the surgery, the epidural caused me to feel like I could not breathe. All I could say was I could not breathe. I thought I was going to die. Shortly after my son was born, I was given a sedative and blacked out and woke up and blacked out again until the surgery was over. My son was in the NICU for respiratory distress at another hospital. I was not allowed to see him for over 36 hours due having a cesarean and his respiratory issues. I was devastated. I never thought that I would be having a cesarean, those only happen for emergencies to save the baby not to save the mother. In the weeks that followed my son's birth I did not realize that I was deeply depressed.

About six months after my son's birth I started to research having a VBAC. I realized that it would be a good option to try for a vaginal birth with my next pregnancy. I decided that I wanted to have a natural childbirth with as little interventions as possible to help me have a natural childbirth as inventions can lead to cesarean surgery. During this time, I found ICAN, the International Cesarean Awareness Network. I joined the online forums and attended local meetings. The support of the women at ICAN was what I needed to not feel alone in my birth journey. They helped my through the emotional pain of my cesarean and helped my with figuring out what I wanted from my next birth experience.

I got pregnant the first month we tried and I miscarried with that pregnancy. I quickly got pregnant again two months later and began prenatal care with an OB that is VBAC friendly. She approved my birth plan. At 39 weeks I went into labor. I called my doula and had her come over to my house to labor until we thought I was close to transition. The day before I was 4 cm dilated and 90% effaced. My contractions started 2 minutes apart and stayed there throughout my labor. After five hours and more intense contractions I decided to go to the hospital.

Once at the hospital, I was given a room and a nurse. The nurse proceeds to go through paperwork and hospital protocols for VBAC. I was told I had to sign a cesarean consent form upon admittance, just in case a cesarean was needed. I refuse to sign the form just in case as I was able to sign when I was in labor with my first. I saw no reason to give them consent to a surgery that was unwanted and not needed.

After that the nurse told me I had to lie in bed so she could hear the baby's heartbeat on the monitor. It was very difficult to stay in bed. The nurse was unable to keep the baby's heart rate on the monitor and was unwilling to work with me so I could remain as comfortable as possible during labor. She continued to pressure me to stay in bed to monitor the baby's heart rate. This continued throughout my labor. She was unwilling help me manage labor pains, she was only concerned about the baby's heart rate which was always fine.

After a while she started pressuring me to break my bag of water so they could start internal monitoring. I declined this intervention knowing that I did not want any invention done just because it is hospital protocol for a VBAC. She pressured me several times as well as my support team to get me to change my mind. There was no indication that an internal monitor was needed to monitor the baby.

The doctor suggested pitocin to strength my contractions as there were not as effective as they should be to get the baby out. I declined knowing that using pitocin during a VBAC labor could increase my chance of a uterine rupture which would result in an emergency cesarean and possible death of the baby and me. The nurse kept pushing the idea of the pitocin and I kept declining as

I was not willing to risk a uterine rupture just for a vaginal birth.

After 20 hours and 5 hours of pushing, my daughter was born by repeat cesarean for failure to progress. She never descended into the birth canal. During the surgery the surgeon noted she was in a military presentation, with her chin up instead to tucked. It is very unlikely that she could have been born vaginally in that position.

I believe that the constant interference from the hospital staff did not allow me to labor in a natural way that I had wanted. I was constantly being told what to do and not allowed to let my body take the lead in labor.

If I have another child, I will plan for a vaginal birth. There are risks to VBAC and repeat cesareans. Risks for a 3rd cesarean include .9% chance of a hysterectomy, 2.26% of blood transfusion, and .57% chance of placenta accrete according to the Silver and Landon study published in Obstetrics & Gynecology in 2006. According to a study by Landon in 2006, the rate of uterine rupture for women with multiple cesareans was .9% and .7% for women with a single cesarean. For me, the risks of a repeat cesarean out ways the risks of a VBAC.

Chapter 24
Emma and Hannah

by Kristine Fordahl Dorrain

Emma's Birth Story

I conceived my daughter in June 2006—a planned pregnancy. My due date was March 23, 2007. In mid-August I was "rear-ended" by another car on my way to work. I experienced some cramping that day and ended up having an early sonogram to verify that the baby was fine. She was not only fine, but very healthy and active and was doing a lot of "acrobatics." The tech snapped a measurement in the middle of a big "stretch," noting that they rarely got a shot of a baby that wasn't all curled up at that stage. The results were sent to my obstetrician, who determined that, based on the baby's size, my due date was two weeks earlier. My first mistake was accepting the statement that "early ultrasound was the most accurate predictor of due dates"—I knew there was no way I conceived when they said I did, but didn't realize at the time how significant my silence would become.

I was told early in my pregnancy that scar tissue due to a previous cryosurgery was a potential problem. I was told by my obstetrician that she might have to break it.

About mid-way through my pregnancy my husband and I attended birthing classes at the hospital we had chosen for the birth. We were eagerly anticipating a "natural" birth without pain medications but learned as much as possible about possible interventions "just in case." I would call us "educated" about birth and our options, but not "wise" as to the ways of hospitals, obstetricians, and labor and delivery wards. After our hospital tour, where the "all-in-one rooms" with private bathtubs for laboring were showcased as a key feature of the hospital, I prepared my birth plan and headed in for my monthly appointment.

As I shared my birth plan with my doctor, she first informed me that all first time moms are taken in by the "suites" as they were called, but that those were for "moms who had delivered seven babies and had proven to be just fine." She wanted me "within seconds of the operating room" for my first baby "just in case." I was disappointed but not daunted. I excitedly showed her my wishes for a medication-free "natural" birth, indicating that, of course, I was reasonable and would agree to medication if I decided I couldn't handle it. She immediately countered with: "There is no need to have a painful birth. You do not need to be a hero. There is no contest as far as who has put up with the most pain in birth." She went to say: "If you do not have a epidural, you will be panicking and screaming and you won't hear a word I say when it's time to push. If you have the epidural, I will say 'You're having a contraction now…it's time to push.' And you will say, 'Ok, Doctor, how was that…should I push harder?' It will be calmer and things will go more smoothly." I was stunned. I tried to tell her I wasn't saying I refused an epidural, but that I wanted to try it without. She made it clear that was not a good choice. My husband chimed in that he didn't want to see me suffer and that he thought her points made sense.

I left that appointment in tears—I felt my doctor was completely unsupportive and I knew at that moment that I wasn't going to have the birth I was planning. My husband interpreted her words as being words of wisdom and experience. He really didn't want to see me in pain and was up for anything that would ensure a positive experience for us both. I felt attacked; he felt like she had our best interests at heart.

In spite of my extreme reservations, I continued to see this doctor.

At my "37 week" (actually, 35 week) appointment, the doctor was concerned that there had been no cervical changes yet. During her exams for each week after that, she tried to push her finger through the scar tissue on my cervix. Each attempt was very painful. In retrospect, I believe she was attempting to strip my membranes. At "39 weeks" she asked me to start prostaglandin gels to soften that tissue. I had gels every day or two (usually twice a day) for two weeks. The gels made me SUPER sensitive to touch internally, and, since I was essentially getting an internal "exam" twice (once before the gel and once during) every day or two I was just raw and sore. I also had to be "admitted" and lie hooked up to monitors for two hours every time they give a dose.

At "40 weeks" my OB wanted to schedule an induction and I refused. At "41 weeks" I agreed to do one at the end of the 41st week. I was told that when I was admitted they would first give me "a little pill on my cervix" to try to start labor (little did I know of the danger!). Then, if that didn't work they would give me an epidural and break the tissue, (epidural first because the process is VERY painful). Meanwhile, the only way the doctor was ok waiting till the end of my "41st week" was because 1. That date was STILL ahead of my original due date and 2. I agreed to a biophysical profile.

The biophysical profile showed that my baby had plenty of amniotic fluid, was nice and chubby, and was very healthy, with no signs of placental deterioration. She was also Posterior. The day of the BPP, my obstetrician looked over the results and wrote up an order for induction. She noted that my cervix was effacing and anterior because there is a scorecard they use for determining if a woman is "ready" for induction and it needed to equal a certain score.

We scheduled the induction for 7 am on Thursday, March 22, 2007. I lay awake all night. I was filled with a sense of dread that this was the start of what would ultimately lead to a c-section. I had no one to talk to. I had never taken the time to really tell my husband or his cousin (a former L&D nurse who was acting as our doula) what my intentions were and how I needed them to advocate for me. I thought I would be fine advocating for myself. And, ultimately, I believed that the doctors only had my (and my baby's) best interests at heart and that they really wouldn't recommend anything unnecessary.

I showed up on time for the induction, armed with copies of my birth plan and a postpartum plan. Upon admitting me, hospital staff started Cytotek immediately. The examining nurse noted with disapproval that there was no way my "scores" on the induction scorecard made me a likely candidate for induction. She could barely reach my cervix. At no point did anyone ever tell me Cytotek was being used "off label" and was not FDA approved for induction purposes. Every 4 or however many hours, there was another dose of Cytotek and more monitoring, followed by lots of walking and intermittent monitoring. They started not allowing me to eat and drink by the end of the first day. By evening I was contracting due to dehydration, but they can't give Cytotek if there more than so many contractions per hour, so they hooked up an IV to get fluids in me to slow the contractions so they could continue the Cytotek.

At 1 pm Friday (Cytotek continued around the clock) my own OB came on duty. She came in and said "what are you doing still here-we need to get things moving." She examined me, told me to breathe, and without warning shoved her finger through my cervix, ripping open the tissue. I recall getting tunnel vision, searing pain, thinking I was dying, and hearing a distant voice screaming and screaming. My husband turned white. I guess I was arched off the bed with only the top of my head and heels touching. It turns out I was the one screaming. There was blood everywhere. She pulled her hand out and said "well, you're a 2 now." She then tried to go back in and break my water. I was sobbing and in shock and nearly crawled off the table. She ordered an epidural. They came in within minutes (waiting around the corner?) and gave me one and then broke my water. I was immediately started on Pitocin. I was in so much shock that it didn't occur to me to refuse. I slept for about three hours, waking only to be "rotated" periodically. After 3 hours I had maybe dilated another centimeter (though there was disagreement about that). My obstetrician bustled in and told me "you are such a hero, you can stop now, you've tried so hard...you're just not going into labor." I was exhausted after 30+ hours without significant sleep and nearly 24 hours without food or water. She convinced me to have a c-section. I sobbed as I signed the consent, knowing that I didn't NEED one. Everyone reassured me it was for the best, but I didn't know why.

An "emergency" c-section came in so I was given a chance to rest some more for a few hours. Just before 9 pm, I was wheeled into the operating room. My doula was there while Mike got ready. Within ten minutes of his arrival, the anesthesiologist told him "Stand up, your baby is being born." I was so nervous and was just shaking. A few seconds later my baby was held up over the screen for me to see, then whisked off to the waiting NICU team (the NICU handles all c-section babies "after hours" because the regular staff has gone home). My husband says it took a minute for them to get her to breathe but when she did, she cried loudly. She was covered in vernix. In fact, it was so thick she couldn't open her eyes.

She was wrapped up and they unstrapped one of my arms so I could "hold" her in an awkward way for a few pictures. I felt weird, like this was not my baby and this was not what being a mom should feel like. I didn't feel any sort of emotion about her. Then I felt very lightheaded and shaky and thought I might pass out—I asked my husband to take her away from me. The anesthesiologist gave me something for that. The baby team and my husband left with Emma. Our doula stayed with me. It was very comforting to have her near me while they stitched me up. She went with me to the recovery room.

When nearly an hour had passed and no one had brought me my baby, I asked her to go tell them to bring her. She came back with my husband and the baby right away and immediately put Emma to my breast. I was pretty drugged up and couldn't really hold her well, but Emma immediately tried to nurse while our doula held her to my breast.

I recovered beautifully from the c-section. I was off all prescription meds besides Tylenol 3 within 24-36 hours of the birth and really only continued to take meds to help control the pain from breastfeeding due to some initial latch issues (that I was too drugged to notice the first couple of attempts at breastfeeding). My physical scar healed without incident and is barely noticeable.

Not one person involved in Emma's birth was in any way hostile to me. Everyone was kind and understanding and almost patronizing. Yet they knew the words to say to "convince" my intelligent, well-read mind that I needed to comply with their suggestions. I think if people had been hostile, it would have been easier to second-guess their intentions and advice. It would have been easier to remember that I was the customer and the decisions were really MY decisions to be making. Instead, the power was theirs because I allowed them to tell me when I could and couldn't move around, eat, etc. They "let me" do things. I didn't make a choice to do them. Just as the blanket assumption that "hospitals are bad places that force their wishes on people" is false, so is the assumption that every doctor and nurse is acting from a place of complete understanding of all available research and "purely out of the best interests for the patient/baby" with complete disregard to their professional reputation. Frequently, hospital staff allow OCOG and other "guidelines" or "policies" to guide their decision making without realizing what is best for individual families or situations. I urge anyone who reads my story to realize the danger of the "cascade of interventions," to educate themselves with the statistics and the data and bring that information with them, and to train their labor support people to advocate for them just as they would advocate for themselves. The goal of all women should not be for a specific birth story, but for an "empowered birth" where they feel the choices were theirs to make and were made, in fact, by them, with the knowledge and data available at the time.

After Emma was home I was paralyzed by fear. She was a high-needs baby and cried if she was ever not in our arms. I struggled to breastfeed…it took nearly a full 30 days for the two of us to get it. Nights blurred into days as I dozed and nursed around the clock. I didn't shower, I didn't get out. I cried for hours, usually in secret so no one would know. I wondered why I didn't "love" my baby like others did. I took "do you have postpartum depression" quizzed online and scored "just fine" on all of them. I was drowning in exhaustion and fatigue and spent days and night re-writing my birth story with a "better outcome." One where I was in charge.

Healing and Preparing for Hannah

I sobbed when I heard of others who had a vaginal birth. I felt overwhelmed. My feelings of failure compounded when I went back to work at 3 months and left my baby behind with my competent husband, who promptly took her on outings, beginning with my first day back. Sex was very traumatic. It was painful, and no one had told me it would hurt. My husband tried to be gentle. We tried everything. My body had failed me and was continuing to fail me. My mind recreated the "birth rape" I had experienced and I sobbed my way through sex. It became easier to just say no.

My husband wanted more kids, but not only could I physically not handle sex, I was terrified of another birth. I started to study VBAC. I learned about homebirth and knew instinctively that was what I wanted. I read Pushed a cried and raged. I read The Thinking Women's Guide to a Better Birth and continued the raging. I was angry.

About the time Emma was 18 months, I woke up one day and it was as if someone took a pair of very dark sunglasses off. It was very odd, this feeling. I figured out that I was happy and not panicking. At that point, I began to realize that I had been depressed. Coming out of it made me see just how dark it was.

Somewhere in there, I attended a Healing Birth Stories workshop. It was the first time I got to sit with other women who were grieving their experiences. I got to hear about people whose births I envied lament their stories. (I wondered "what are you doing here"?) I got to hear from women who were lucky their babies lived. (I thought "you should be thankful to have a healthy baby.") Then I realized that we were all there because people were telling us how to feel about an experience that had not been what we'd planned for and hoped for. We'd all had our dreams dashed. While we all had healthy babies, that wasn't the point. We were all suffering. I stopped judging and started listening. I don't really remember what happened that day. I know there were candles and a ceremony. I just remembered that I felt like someone finally "got it." I finally felt heard. I felt like I was part of a community.

I went to Birth Video night. I wanted video after video of homebirths and cried. I was so jealous and felt so robbed. I deserved to have a peaceful birth too!

Sometime after that I felt like I was ready to try again. I made it clear to my husband that it was homebirth or no birth. It was not optional. We conceived on the first try. The physical pain of sex had faded, but the emotional pain was there still. I was relieved it took one try, he was disappointed.

True to form, I began to plan. I made lists. I had a three-page questionnaire for interviewing midwives. I read and re-read birth books. I enrolled in a Birthing from Within Class for me and a Bradley class for my husband. I attended ICAN meetings. I exposed my fears in front of others…I cried. I told my husband and our classmates that I thought he would let me down…that he would succumb to the siren song of medical interventions and drag me to to the hospital when I was at my weakest, unable to resist. I told him I was devastated that we weren't on the same page for our first birth. I thought he was ignoring me.

The Birth Story of Hannah

On Tuesday, September 29th, I attended our next-to-last Bradley class, where we went through a "long labor" scenario—little did I know how prophetic it was. I had been having uncomfortable cramping all day, and figured it was really early stuff and didn't get too excited about it. Wednesday, I woke up with more consistent cramps and decided to go to work. Why not? Better than lying around the house, hoping for progress. I cleaned off my desk before I left, pretty sure that things weren't going to get any more comfortable overnight. I was right. I went to bed with Emma and we fell asleep at 10 pm. As I was going to bed, I told Mike "go to sleep. I think we'll be up later." At 12:15 am, the contractions woke me up. I tried to go back to sleep, but couldn't, so I got up and went downstairs…Mike was still up. I said the contractions hurt and that maybe he should fill the birth tub. He was bummed that he hadn't slept.

I tried to rest on the couch and the recliner, but couldn't get comfortable. I had to concentrate through the contractions (which never really seemed to "build"…they just started out with a bang and tapered off, so they were constantly sneaking up on me). I purposely didn't time them. Mike set up the tub and we called our doula, Rebecca P (who had "had a feeling" so was sleeping on her couch). We agreed to connect in the morning as I felt I was ok without her at that point. Mike continued to set things up and then went up to nap because Emma was likely to wake up looking for one of us. He was upstairs from about 5 am to about 8 am. During that time, I tried to rest, but was extremely uncomfortable and the contractions just kept sneaking up on me. I only had a digital clock and estimated the contractions at 5-7 minutes apart, lasting approx. a minute. At some point early in the morning, I vomited, a precursor of what was to come.

About 6 am, I called my mom to come get Emma and our midwife, Jeanne Bazille. Jeanne had another mom whose water had broken and thought she'd go there first if I didn't feel like I needed her right away. I didn't. I called Rebecca who started to get ready to come—again, no rush.

When Mike and Emma got up, we timed the contractions at 5 minutes apart and lasting a minute. My mom showed up for Emma, and Rebecca came around noon. I couldn't talk through the contractions, but felt like I was relatively chatty between them. I wasn't hungry, but did try to drink water as much as possible. I started to vomit whatever I ate so we started experimenting with foods that might stay down. Rebecca was a wealth of ideas. I walked, sat, lay on the couch, stood, sat on the toilet, and climbed stairs. The tub felt the best of all, and actually helped the contractions space out a tiny bit.

Jeanne came that evening, on her way back from the other birth. The contractions were intense and coming every 2-4 minutes—still sneaking up on me. Sometimes I would have two in a row, with no break. She talked about more techniques to get labor moving with Rebecca and I asked for a cervical check. She could barely reach my cervix and thought I might be dilated to between 2-4, but wasn't sure. I was a little discouraged, but felt like the night would bring a lot of progress. She left and Rebecca and Mike took turns all night helping me with the contractions and napping.

Friday morning, Jeanne and her apprentice, Erin both came. I had continued to vomit, so Jeanne checked my ketones. The strip was purple—I really needed food and water. They started an "eat and drink" campaign and the goal was to keep as much in for as long as possible before vomiting. Between contractions, I had a bite of something and drank water, Emergen-C, whatever they could find. I was back in the tub in some very deep squat-like positions, trying to get baby to work her way down and the contractions were intense. Again, they seemed to just keep hitting like a Mack truck without warning and many were "doubles" or even "triples." We checked my ketones again and the strip showed only a trace! Success!

I was exhausted by 2 pm and we decided to see if there had been any progress. My cervix had come forward and was reachable, but I was still only about 2 cm dilated. The progress made in about 36 hours of labor, especially the 16 hours since the last check was so minimal, I was very discouraged. We started to discuss transferring to the hospital while I was still in relatively good shape. I could get IV fluids and glucose to give me energy. I was talking about getting an epidural so I could take a nap. We decided if I waited much longer, any trip to the hospital would be more likely to result in a repeat c-section, so we decided to go. It was 3 pm on Friday, 39 hours from when I had last slept (for 2 hours).

We got to the hospital around 4pm and they were ready for us. They checked me pretty quickly once I got there (my bag of waters was still intact) and we found that the car ride (which was its own hell) had somehow got me dilated to 5cm; we were all very encouraged. But then the contractions started rolling, one on top of the other. I quickly lost all ability to focus. We got the IV fluids quite quickly and by the time ½ a bag was in me, I felt a lot better, but the contractions only picked up in intensity. I was not coping well; mostly due to fatigue.

The first doctor to come in said that she recommended a repeat c-section. We disagreed and she called the consulting OB, who came in and said the same thing (during a contraction!). They started with the drama of my scar thinning and not holding up. While they didn't exactly say "exploding uterus" the OB was worried that, if I let things go too far that "there would be nothing left to stitch up (I believe she said "cheesecloth") when you did need a c-section." In my pain and exhaustion, I started to hear "you won't have a uterus, your baby might be in danger, there will be nothing we can do." The doctors left so my team and I could talk.

We recognized the doctor's concern, but Mike was insistent that I could do it. Every time I had said I couldn't do it anymore, I had kept on doing it, and he believed that I could. He had heard me during our Birthing from Within and Bradley classes saying that I wish I had clearly communicated my birth wishes to him so that he could advocate for me. He had heard me say that my greatest fear was that I would give up and he wouldn't help me fight. He saw the depression and trauma over Emma's birth and was determined that this birth would not be the same. Between contractions we argued and talked. He worried that a c-section would mess with my head so badly I'd never be myself again. I worried that my uterus wouldn't make it through more labor AND and possible c-section. Eventually I admitted that I didn't believe my uterus would explode and that we'd give my body time to work since it was trying to do its job. He agreed to the epidural so I could rest and take a break.

The anesthesiologist was great. The epidural was perfect. I could feel my feet and even could turn myself over in bed or lift my hips off the bed. I still felt a lot of back and tailbone pressure and contractions, but I was able to get some rest. I napped. When I awoke, I commented on my long nap. Everyone joked that I had only slept for 45 minutes, but I felt great! At the time of the epidural, I was dilated to "between 6-7."

I could feel the baby working its way down. An hour after the epidural, I was checked again and we were disappointed (but not really shocked) to find no progress, but a bulging bag of waters. The nurse suggested rupturing my membranes. Meanwhile, the OB came back in and very brusquely recommended an immediate c-section. I said that I wanted one more hour to progress and then we would talk. She asked me "are you declining a c-section against medical advice?" I said "yes." We agreed to rupture the membranes and do internal monitoring. The entire time, the external monitor kept coming off, kept giving really erratic readings, and often someone had to hold it in place. Even the "good readings" were somewhat alarming to those watching and we wanted to accurately know how baby was holding up to everything (since she'd been working all this time too!).

The charge nurse came in to break the water and insert the monitors and I turned over. She started to insert the monitors, thinking the instruments would break the bag and found that my water had broken spontaneously just before that. The internal monitors showed that baby was fine. The water was clear and I breathed a sigh of relief that baby was handling the stress well.

An hour later I was dilated to 8 cm and everyone was pleased. The nurses were very encouraging, telling me I would soon be pushing my baby out. An hour later, I was complete on the left side (I was lying on my left side) with a lip on the right. The nurse flipped me to my right side and positioned my left leg up on the table with a pillow. She called this "the running man" and said that it would help get baby into position.

About 20 minutes later I started to bear down with the contractions. It took a bit for me to figure out I was pushing and Jeanne asked me "are you pushing"? I said I thought so and worried about pushing on an incomplete cervix. She said if my body was doing it, to just let it. I lay there, pushing and resting for about an hour. The epidural pump started to beep, notifying us that it was empty. The nurse had told me I should let her know when I wanted to push. Eventually she saw that I sort of WAS pushing and asked "are you ready"? I decided I was. There was a lot of pressure so I pushed the bolus for the epidural. The nurse said it was empty and that I could let it just wear off or get more. My team encouraged me that feeling the pushing would help so I made a decision to just drop the button and get to work.

A mirror was brought in and the nurse was awesome. My whole team was there to hold my legs and help me learn how to push, offering a lot of GREAT suggestions. The nurse was a little worried about the baby's heart rate and asked me to really push hard, three times with each contraction. She stood back and watched as Rebecca and Jeanne helped me push and Erin and Mike held my legs. Everyone was cheering and it felt great to push!

They had to call a doctor to "catch" the baby and a very young resident showed up. I was hoping I could get the baby out for Jeanne to catch, but it didn't work out. I loved watching my baby crown! Everyone was encouraging me to push slowly as she crowned but it was like a Mack truck screaming through my body just pushing her out! Her head was born and her shoulders slid right out in the same contraction. As they placed her on me, I was in awe…I had DONE IT! I had birthed my baby vaginally!!! I wasn't broken.

She looked like Emma when she came out. Everyone was rubbing her and the doctor was pushing my belly to get the placenta out and Rebecca reminded me to feel the pulsing of the cord. It was kind of crazy. The nurse, who had requested my birth plan, and apparently, read it, reminded the doctor not to cut the cord right away and knew all of my wishes. They didn't take her away for an hour and half, then took her only to another corner of the room to weigh/measure her while I took a quick bath.

Hannah was born at St. John's at 2:15 am on October 3, 2009 after 50 hours of labor (one hour of active pushing). About an hour after her birth I asked if we could go home, I felt that good.

Epilogue:

The glow from Hannah's birth has continued into her second year. I didn't experience any postpartum depression, but the anxiety was still there, especially early on. I panicked about being alone with both girls. I discovered The Mood Cure and began taking supplements. After about 3 months, I was dramatically more stable. We are considering another child and, if so, will be planning another homebirth. I still cry over my first birth and I was a little surprised that my heart can grieve the first birth and thrill over the second at the same time.

Chapter 25
My Miscarriage Story
by Rebecca Bolton-Steiner

I was due with my third baby right around the same time as my other kids' birthdays. My sister was due at the same time as I was, so we did this whole pregnancy together. We were so excited. When I was almost 15 weeks pregnant, I woke up in the morning and went to the bathroom and there was some blood, and it wasn't like dried old blood, it was bright red.

In the morning I called my clinic and went in for an ultrasound. The ultrasound tech said, "I'm just really sorry to tell you that there's no heartbeat and it looks like–" and I was between fourteen to fifteen weeks and she says, "It looks like the size of like a nine-week baby," and I was like, "Okay," and my first reaction was just sort of, "Okay, well, now we know, okay, now what," and then I just freaked out about my sister. I felt the floor drop out from under me. I just like started sobbing and said, "Oh my God, what about my sister?"

After the ultrasound I had an appointment with one of the midwives, and she said, "So you're just going to go home and do this by yourself" and I said, "Yeah, I guess." I was never offered anything, they never said, "We can do a D&C;" they never said, we can give you medicine, they never said there was anything I could do other than just go home and do it by myself. And she said

247

about being pregnant with twins that she had some bleeding early on, so she sort of knew how I felt. I remember clearly remember thinking that was odd, that someone else would be really hurt and offended by that. And now I'm hurt and offended by it, but at the time, it was just sort of– I was sort of blown away by the whole thing, like I couldn't believe she actually said that to somebody who had just been told that wouldn't have a baby.

The next day I was feeling crampy but nothing major. I was on the toilet and a bunch of stuff fell out of me, and I looked and there was a little fetus and it looked very alien, like it didn't look very formed but it also didn't look very decayed and I remember just being like I wasn't really ready to see that, like I wasn't–I expected more of a baby given where I was, and it hadn't developed past sort of that like embryonic alien face. My husband took care of it and I got in the tub. I remember everybody saying if you bleed too much, you should go get seen, but I never really knew what too much meant. Was it "I'm feeling more than a pad an hour, we should probably go in."? I didn't think it would be like all of a sudden I was bleeding too much, and I had no reference for how much too much was, especially because I was in the water, you know, I was in the bathtub.

So I drained the bathtub and I stood up and was trying to shower off and blood is just gushing out of me and I went to lay down. I wasn't feeling physically unsafe or dizzy or anything like that. I really was feeling okay, and after awhile I said, "You know, I should probably check my pad because it's been awhile, I should check my pad." I stood up and I got out of the bed. I got to the doorway, not very far, and felt something drop out of me and then like spatter on the floor. I looked down and it was a football-sized clot. "I'm okay, I'm okay," and I got to the bathroom and I said, "I don't feel very good," and my husband came running in the bathroom. I passed out in the bathtub, and he apparently caught my head before I hit the bathtub. I remember him trying to get me to talk to him and say the ABCs. I remember him telling my sister to call 911.

We got to the hospital, and my mom, my two doulas, my midwife were there. The nurse kept telling everyone that they need to leave. And I said, "Well, are they in your way?" I was so scared of being alone. They had to put another IV on me in the ER and I was so thirsty, I just wanted something to drink and she kept saying, "no, we might have to do a D&C, you can't have had anything," and she was just like crabby at me the whole time and she was acting like I couldn't do anything right and I just remember being really confused, thinking, "what am I doing wrong? what can I be doing to change how she's being? I'm obviously doing something wrong here because otherwise she wouldn't be mean to me." I'm really scared of needles and she just wasn't compassionate about that at all, so she was just jabbing things in my arm. They had to draw blood for some reason-- and I made some dumb joke about how, couldn't they just use the blood that was gushing out of me or something like that, and she didn't think it was funny. It was very offensive, I said something else about how–I made some other dumb joke about something like I'm not bleeding enough, you have to take more blood or something like that, and she said, "well if you don't want us to take blood, then I guess we can just let you keep bleeding" or something. I don't think you can really tell people who are delirious– yell at them for what they're saying.

At one point the nurse came in and said that they needed to do an ultrasound to see if they were going to have to do a D&C. I didn't even really know what a D&C was at that point. I remember saying, "okay, we can do an ultrasound" instead of "why would we need to do a D&C" and she said, "well if you would just stop bleeding, we wouldn't have to even be talking about it." I just remember feeling like it's not my fault, I don't know how to make it stop, you know, like a voluntary action. I'm not trying to bleed to death, and I passed out. I don't even know how many times in the ER actually on the table, and I would get really, really hot and jittery right before I would pass out, like I could feel it coming, like I was feeling like someone was like pressing on my chest. I'd say, "I'm going to pass out, I'm going to pass out, I'm going to pass out!" and she'd say, "You're fine, you're already laying down, I just felt like that was really not a very nice thing to say.

And I remember my midwife saying nobody ever assessed my bleeding while I was in the ER and I remember her saying, "She's bleeding a lot, we should probably check her padding" or something like that, and

250

the nurse saying, "She's got plenty of pads, I'm not worried about the bed." Yeah, she was a total bitch.

I'd pass out and they'd drop the head of the bed at an angle and then they'd put it back flat, and they'd drop it again the next time I passed out.

Eventually some orderly came in to get me to take me down to the room for the D&C. The orderly said, "We can't have anyone with you when we do it." I said, "Why?" and he says, "Well, there's just no room for anybody else," I said, "Well, I can't be alone," and he says, "Well, [your doula] can come down the hall with us but I can't let her in the room." My doula was walking with me and I said–"Something else just came out of me, something big, like I just passed another clot. " My doula said, "This is ridiculous, I'm looking at how much blood you have when we get in there," and I said "Okay," because nobody had checked my bleeding at that point and the orderly said, "I can't let you in the room," and I said, "Why," and he said, "Well, I'm just not supposed to," and I said, "I need someone to be in there with me, I don't want to be my myself," and he says, "I understand," and I said, "She's coming in with me," and he said okay. We got in there and he kept saying there's no room in there; there's not going to be any room in there. The room was huge.

I found out later that it says in my chart that I refused a D&C, and it says that I declined something, either Pitocin or methergine in the ER, that I declined it and that I refused to have my hemoglobin tested. At this point, I'm seeing blood pressure numbers that probably mean I'm dead, under 30 for the bottom number .It says I declined a whole bunch of shit that they never even offered me. I'm bleeding and I know enough about bleeding out of your uterus that I should have had Pit in my bag. Immediately. I should have the lactated ringers, and I just had the straight saline. Maybe if I didn't know any of that, I wouldn't feel like I was so neglected. But knowing that they have a medicine that contracts your uterus, and that they didn't give it to me… There's no baby to hurt; there's no birth to mess with.

Then they were going to send me home, and I remember being panicked and confused about that. "Okay, well, does that mean I'm done bleeding then?" and she said, "Yeah, if you soak more than a pad an hour you should come back," and I said, "Okay, so I'm not bleeding that much anymore," and she said, "No," and she sat me up and pulled the IV out. No fanfare, just pulled it out. I'm trickling blood because you don't gush blood when you have none. I think she said my hemoglobin was ten at that point, which is almost normal, it's low, it should be eleven-ish, twelve-ish, but I was 14 weeks pregnant, so it's a little low anyway. If someone bleeds a whole bunch and you test the blood that's still in their body it isn't accurate. It was a lot lower than that later.

The nurse said "Well, your hemoglobin is fine," and she sat me up, pulled out the IV, and I passed out. She would sit me up and I would feel like I was underwater, like a hollow ringing kind of thing, and really dizzy and I'd be like, "I'm going to pass out, I'm going to pass out, I'm going to pass out!" and then I'd pass out. That happened like three or four times. I was also super hot and I'd try and take off all of my–I had a robe on over me, and I'd try and take off all my clothes. She was pushing them back on me and telling me I couldn't be naked in front of them. "You don't want to be naked in front of all these people," and I'm saying, "Just shut the door," and she said, "We can't shut the door because of the air flow." She had a reason that nothing I wanted was ever going to be the thing that could happen. She was just so mean to me, and–I didn't necessarily know it then, but I really feel like she was being intentionally mean, like now, looking at it after the fact... she took my IV out before she took my blood pressure again, you know what I mean? So then I had to get another IV, and then she sat me up, like more than once after I had already passed out. It doesn't make any sense from what I know about care in general, the only way I can explain it is that she was doing it intentionally. It seem like more than just neglect.

I started wondering if I was having unrealistic expectations. Maybe they're not nice to people just in general. I was all delusional thinking maybe if they were nice to you it was worse. This was for your best; this was for your own good. Like being a total asshole to me was somehow good for me or something.

And somehow, at some point they got me moved up to labor and delivery where I got to listen to all the babies cry, but at least once I was up on labor and delivery, they were so nice to me. The labor and delivery nurse came in, and she hugged me and said, "I'm so sorry about the baby; I know you wanted that baby," and that was the first time anybody ever said there was a baby, ever acknowledged that I had a miscarriage. She said, "Well, I asked–I was talking to your doctor and I asked her if she wanted me to give you methergine," and I was a little bit like put off, I wasn't really sure I wanted to take anything, and then she says, "Well, I asked your doctor if she wanted me to give you methergine," and I was like, "Oh, ding, this was your idea and not my doctor, yeah," and at that point I said, "Okay," I totally felt comfortable with it because I felt like the nurse was actually taking care of me, She was the first person who actually took care of me- other than the people who I snuck in, who weren't supposed to be there.

The next morning they came in and said that I needed to have a blood transfusion. I said, "I am going to need some time to talk to my family about this," and she said, "Well, you're going to have to decide now," and I said, "I can decide in a couple minutes, right?" It was like I need to do everything right now. She huffed and puffed and left and then she said, "Your other option is you could sign out AMA," and I said, "No, I don't think I'll be doing that."

I guess they wanted me to do something before it had been 24 hours that I'd been in the hospital because they have to change your admission status at 24 hours. Once I figured out that it was all like a fucking timing game with them, I was realized that I didn't need to do this anymore. You don't need a decision from me, you just need to figure out how to fill out your fucking paperwork. It just came down to I was paperwork, I was nothing else to them, and my doctor couldn't even be bothered to come down to the hospital to see me to check on me, so I declined the blood transfusion.

When I was getting discharged, I said, "So should I come in and get my hemoglobin checked at some point," and she says, "Yeah, you can just follow up with your primary doctor," and I said, "So I shouldn't come into the clinic," and she said no. I was just completely dropped by my clinic; they just completely dropped me.

About the Author

Maureen Campion, M.S.,LP loves blending her own personal experiences as a mom with her professional training as a psychologist to help people build amazing relationships and strong families. She lives and works in the Twin Cities and loves Facebook for connecting with people around the world.

maureen@marriagegeek.com

Marriagegeek.com

Healyourbirthstory.com

Facebook.com/marriagegeek

Facebook.com/healyourbirthstory

Thank you Kollin Leisinger at Nonstudio Design + Print for the cover art. nonstudios@gmail.com

References

Beck, C., & Driscoll, J. (2013). Traumatic childbirth. Abingdon, Oxon: Routledge.

Kendall-Tackett, K. (1994). Postpartum Depression. Illness, Crisis, & Loss, 80-86.

Madsen, L. (1994). Rebounding from childbirth: Toward emotional recovery. Westport, Conn.: Bergin & Garvey.

Made in the USA
Monee, IL
11 January 2022